T0133787

SUCCESSFUL SCRUMBUTT

LEARN TO MODIFY SCRUM PROJECT MANAGEMENT
FOR STUDENT AND VIRTUAL TEAMS

SUCCESSFUL SCRUMBUTT

LEARN TO MODIFY SCRUM PROJECT MANAGEMENT FOR STUDENT AND VIRTUAL TEAMS

NOAH DYER

CRC Press
Taylor & Francis Group
Boca Raton London New York

CRC Press is an imprint of the
Taylor & Francis Group, an **informa** business

A FOCAL PRESS BOOK

CRC Press
Taylor & Francis Group
6000 Broken Sound Parkway NW, Suite 300
Boca Raton, FL 33487-2742

© 2016 by Taylor & Francis Group, LLC
CRC Press is an imprint of Taylor & Francis Group, an Informa business

No claim to original U.S. Government works

Printed on acid-free paper
Version Date: 20160805

International Standard Book Number-13: 978-1-138-93098-8 (Paperback)

Library of Congress Cataloging-in-Publication Data

Names: Dyer, Noah, author.
Title: Successful ScrumButt : learn to modify Scrum project management for student and virtual teams / authored by Noah Dyer.
Description: New York : Routledge, 2017. | Includes index.
Identifiers: LCCN 2016025998 | ISBN 9781138930988 (pbk.)
Subjects: LCSH: Scrum (Computer software development) | Project management--Data processing. | Agile software development.
Classification: LCC QA76.76.D47 D943 2017 | DDC 658.4/040285--dc23
LC record available at https://lccn.loc.gov/2016025998

Visit the Taylor & Francis Web site at
http://www.taylorandfrancis.com

and the CRC Press Web site at
http://www.crcpress.com

Printed and bound in the United States of America by
Edwards Brothers Malloy on sustainably sourced paper

Contents

Acknowledgements   *xi*

1
How I Came to Scrum   *1*
   Chapter in a Tweet   *1*
   From Hobby Game Developer to Marketing Agency Partner   *1*
   The Tyranny of the Semester   *5*

2
Why Is Scrum the Solution?   *7*
   Chapter in a Tweet   *7*
   Review of Project Management Problems   *8*
   Non-Scrum Ways of Solving These Problems   *8*
      Detailed Upfront Planning and Estimation   *9*
      Tight Employee Supervision and Hierarchies   *9*
      Team-Building Activities   *9*
      Detailed Contracts and Relationship Managers *10*
      Complex Software for Managing Task Relationships and
      Dependencies   *10*
      Focus Groups   *11*
   Cost-Centric Project Management   *11*
   The Waterfall   *12*
   Return on Investment Focus   *13*
   The Agile Manifesto   *13*
   Individuals and Interactions   *14*
   Working Software   *15*
   Customer Collaboration   *15*
   Responding to Change   *16*

So Many Words, How About Some Pictures?   16
Is Scrum a Solution for Every Project?   17
What Are the Alternatives to Scrum?   18
Why Is It Called Scrum?   18

3
Why ScrumButt   21
  Chapter in a Tweet   21
  I Sense That There's a ~~Butt~~ "But"   23

4
How to Use This Book   25
  Chapter in a Tweet   25

5
The First Secret of Scrum: The Product Owner   29
  Chapter in a Tweet   29
  What Makes a Bad Product Owner?   31
    Multiple Personalities   31
    Indecisive   32
    Unavailable   33
    Irresponsible   33
    Unintuitive   33
    Unrespectable   34
    Technically Minded   35
    Bossy   36
  ScrumButt Modifications   36
  The Bottom Line   36

6
The Second Secret of Scrum: The Product Backlog   39
  Chapter in a Tweet   39
  What's Not on the List?   41
  Release Early, Release Often   42
  Grooming the Product Backlog   43
  AsABIWaB   44
    As a Blank   44
    I Want Blank   46
    So That Blank   46
    Back to Our Example   46

That's Not a Story!   47
The Devil Is in the Details   48
Where Does the Product Backlog Live?   48
Modifications for ScrumButt   49
The Bottom Line   50

7

The Third Secret of Scrum: The Superheroes   53
Chapter in a Tweet   53
Super Diverse   54
Super Leaders, Not Super Bosses   55
Super Competent   55
Super Hideout   56
Super Exclusive   57
Modifications for ScrumButt   58
The Bottom Line   61

8

The Fourth Secret of Scrum: Sprint Planning and Sprint Backlog   63
Chapter in a Tweet   63
The Promise   63
Conversations   64
Capacity   64
Back to Gardening   65
Average Joe Hours   66
Story Points   66
Using Story Points to Determine Capacity   69
How Much Work Should We Estimate?   69
The Estimating Process   69
    Wrong   70
    Wrong, but with AsABIWaB   70
    Right   71
Now It's Time for a Breakdown   72
Definition of Done   73
How Many Beans Are in This Jar?   74
Planning Poker   74
Taking on Work   75
Modifications for ScrumButt   76
The Bottom Line   78

9

The Fifth Secret of Scrum: The ScrumMaster and Scrum Coach   *81*
    Chapter in a Tweet   *81*
    The Supreme Court Justice   *81*
    A Judge Needs Good Judgment   *82*
    More Servant than Master   *83*
    Interruption Interceptor   *84*
    Good Teams Have Good Coaches   *85*
    Modifications for ScrumButt   *85*
    The Bottom Line   *86*

10

The Sixth Secret of Scrum: Daily Stand-Ups   *87*
    Chapter in a Tweet   *87*
    One Day at a Time   *87*
    Why Stand-Up?   *88*
    The Attendees   *88*
    The 3Whatchus   *89*
        Whatchu Done?   *89*
        WhatchuDoin'?   *90*
        Whatchu 'Fraid Of?   *91*
    The Burndown   *91*
    Ahead or Behind   *94*
    The Nuclear Option   *94*
    The Angel Option   *96*
    Modifications for ScrumButt   *97*
    The Bottom Line   *99*

11

The Seventh Secret of Scrum: Sprint Reviews and Retrospectives   *101*
    Chapter in a Tweet   *101*
    The Sprint Review   *101*
        Demonstration   *102*
        Acceptance   *102*
        Influence   *103*
    The Sprint Retrospective   *104*
    Review Velocity   *105*
        Review Prior Retrospective Commitments   *105*
        Start/Continue/Stop   *106*

Commit to Improvements   *107*
   Keep It Up, and Keep It Fresh   *108*
Modifications for ScrumButt   *109*
The Bottom Line   *109*

12
Do It!   *111*
   Chapter in a Tweet   *111*

Glossary   *113*

Index   *115*

Acknowledgements

Thank you to Sean Connelly, Caitlin Murphy, Kristina Ryan, Richard Tressider, and Christine Selvan for their invaluable help in approving, assembling, and editing this book.

Thanks to the game development faculty at UAT for their commitment to join me in bringing scrum to the classroom.

I would like to thank the team at On Advertising, who let me work on this book when I should have been working on other things, and who have also embraced scrum with me.

My family and loved ones were incredibly supportive, and helped me to write more and play video games less.

Most especially I'm thankful for Enoch, Mattie, Linkin, and Lillie, my beautiful babies who keep me practicing the scrum value of dedicating time to the most important things first.

1

How I Came to Scrum

> To paraphrase Oedipus, Hamlet, Lear, and all those guys, "I wish I had known this some time ago."
>
> **Roger Zelazny,** *Sign of the Unicorn*

Chapter in a Tweet

Before scrum, the author was a hot mess, albeit a well-intentioned one.

In order to understand why I love scrum so much, you might find it helpful to know what my business life was like before I found scrum.

From Hobby Game Developer to Marketing Agency Partner

In the early 2000s, my friends and I wanted to make a video game. I had a friend who wanted to be the writer/designer and another friend who wanted to be the artist. I needed to be the programmer.

I'd already earned my bachelor's degree, but by some unfortunate miracle I had never written a line of code.

Over the next couple years, we created documentation for lots of game ideas. We made several prototypes based off these ideas, but never polished and shipped a game. The reasons we didn't ship any games at that time were manifold, but it's worth bringing up a couple of the most important.

First, as an inexperienced team, we had absolutely no concept of scope. We thought we were pursuing simple ideas, but many of those ideas never had a chance at being made by three people in their lifetime.

Second, as we slogged through our coding, art, and design challenges, by the time we got a prototype working, we'd typically lost enthusiasm for the idea or perhaps, more accurately, gained a lot more enthusiasm for some new idea.

So after a couple years, our return on investment (ROI) was –100%, the worst possible ROI you can have. We'd never gained anything for our investment of thousands of hours, other than the inherent learning in our activities. For the record, as a university professor, I certainly recognize the value of learning, but including learning in ROI calculations is counterproductive, because then every single investment is bound to have a return of the knowledge you gained by making it. This gets messy for comparing investments, which is the fundamental purpose of the ROI formula.

> **ROI**—Return on Investment. The notion of comparing how much a thing costs to the benefits derived. The actual formula will be discussed elsewhere.

As new developers, and perhaps not the most astute of business people, the things I just described to you weren't immediately and obviously apparent to us. Instead, we just thought we needed a bigger and better team. We didn't have a network of professional game developers or even other hobbyists that we could reach out to at the time, so if we wanted to grow our team, we were going to have to hire people.

The problem was that none of us had any real money to speak of at that time, and we were too cowardly to ask anyone else for money. We decided to solve our problem in a very roundabout way. We would use our newfound programming and art skills to start Internet businesses, and we would use the proceeds of those businesses to fund our game dreams. What could be simpler!?

Over the next year or so we converted our game dev knowledge to web dev knowledge and built some cool sites and products. We even put a little cash into some of our ideas. Alas, we didn't understand marketing very well, so we generated very little traffic to our sites and subsequent revenue. Our ROI was still very close to –100%, and we didn't have the windfall necessary to grow our team.

In hindsight, it's obvious that our project management process isn't working out so hot. We're not launching the projects we're most excited about, and the projects we do end up launching after a lot of effort aren't resonating with our target customers.

Unfortunately, at the time it didn't dawn on us that project management was our problem, so we kind of put the studio to the side in hopes of coming back to it at some future time after fortune had taken better care of us.

Meanwhile, the people in my network knew that I'd gotten into web development, so I started getting asked to build other people's sites. And because I knew from painful experience that if you build it, people will not necessarily come, I started learning about SEO and other web marketing strategies and offering these services to my clients.

Initially, I billed people hourly for these services, which was a beautiful thing for me. I knew that I was being honest, and I got paid for every hour I worked.

Unfortunately, not every client trusted me as much as I trusted myself. This may stem from the fact that, initially, I was a horrible estimator.

There were lots of reasons for this, and they weren't unique to me. I've found that most developers are horrible at estimating the time it takes to complete a task for their entire career! The majority of the time these poor estimates tend to be too optimistic.

When you horribly estimate the multitude of individual tasks that result in a complete application, the margins of error become huge. It's not uncommon for a project to take two to four times as many hours as was initially estimated, and, alas, I was no exception.

Of course, customers don't like this. They want a fixed number at the start of the project, and I sympathized with this desire. I thought, "Should the customer really have to pay for the fact that I can't reliably estimate a task?"

I concluded that they should not, and that I would begin offering my services at a fixed price. I figured that I would have to take some lumps early on but that taking these lumps would ultimately teach me valuable lessons that would make me a better estimator and allow me to profitably serve all my clients.

Fast forward 6 years or so, I've now graduated from a freelancer, to the COO of a prominent digital marketing agency, to a founding partner of my own marketing agency, which had been open for a few years at this point.

My personal passion for fixed pricing has now become a company passion. I've become a way better estimator personally. More importantly, I've surrounded myself with other competent developers who are even better estimators. But still we're rarely able to make our fixed-price contracts profitable, which are now worth tens and hundreds of thousands of dollars each.

Furthermore, despite the fact that half the time I'm literally paying money out of my pocket to finish our customers' projects at the price they were originally quoted, they frequently still aren't happy with us, because the projects are delivered later than estimated, or because we couldn't agree on a price for a change they requested, or any number of other reasons.

Let me share a typical example. We would begin all projects with a blueprinting phase, for which the customer would pay many thousands of dollars. In this phase, we would do all the graphic design, so people would know what their project was going to look like. We would also plan out all the database structures, the classes, and the functions that would be necessary to drive the website, and the third-party integrations for things like merchant processing, etc. Most importantly, we would write a plain language description of how all these things would work, so that our customer could understand what we were working on.

After several weeks and many revisions, we would drop the final blueprint on the customer's desk. These documents were many dozens of pages, primarily technical in nature. Most important to the customer, the blueprint included a fixed price quote to build the project it described, to which the customer would agree and we'd get to work.

Inevitably, a number of things would happen after we got started. First, the customer would think of some major feature they had completely neglected to consider and want to make a change. Half the time, we would get blamed for not thinking of the feature during blueprinting, and so there was extreme pressure to throw in such features without changing the price.

We were naturally in the position of being resistant to any change big or small, because even a small change could drastically change the architecture of the system, which may have been very nearly complete by this point. And of course, the customer would always feel like we were raking them over the coals when we quoted a large price for a change that in their mind was small.

Another problem we would encounter is that we would get stonewalled by circumstances outside of our control. For example, a credit card company would change its architecture for processing payments but wouldn't properly document the new method, leaving us to experiment in the dark. Or a database that was to be created by the company's internal IT department would be behind schedule, halting our own progress. As the saying goes, what could go wrong, did go wrong.

After accommodating for the client's new requests, and navigating whatever misfortunes were randomly placed in our way, one more thing would nearly always happen. Things would apparently progress on schedule for the many weeks or months of development, except for the last couple weeks before the delivery date. Then, when all of the work was supposed to come together into a coherent whole, new bugs would pop up, things wouldn't work together as anticipated, etc.

Solving these last-minute integration issues always took longer than we budgeted, sometimes weeks or months. The longer it took, the more the company was sacrificing from its profits to deliver according to the fixed price. As you can imagine, customers aren't grateful at this point that you are sacrificing your profits to deliver at your promised price, they are upset that you weren't done when you said you would be.

Are you stressed yet? It's clear things were broken. No matter how much we charged, no matter how much of a buffer we put in, no matter how long we spent in the blueprint phase, things didn't go right nearly often enough.

You may be thinking the problem is that I'm simply a dumb man with a dumb team. While I won't dispute that there may be some truth there, a quick survey proved that others in the industry faced similar challenges. Most of them solved the problem by telling the customer tough luck and billing them hourly. But I knew there had to be a better way that didn't leave the customer with the short end of the stick. Can you guess what it is?

The Tyranny of the Semester

Depending on the experiences you've had prior to and during your education, my own story may not resonate with yours. If that's the case, here's one that may hit a little closer to home.

I used to be a professor of game programming at the University of Advancing Technology. At the time, UAT had over 500 students enrolled in their game development–related degree programs. UAT was proud that it had built a curriculum that frequently allowed students to work on their own passion projects in their classes, rather than having the professors prescribe projects that the students must complete.

While you might occasionally expect a small fraction of students to bomb due to inexperience and other factors, the UAT faculty expected that, by allowing students this freedom, project quality would generally be high because of student engagement and commitment. However, when I arrived, a frequent complaint by both students and faculty was that student projects consistently didn't come together by the end of the semester.

Lots of reasons were observed and suggested as the culprits of this problem. Students frequently just couldn't be made to understand and adopt a reasonable scope for a game that's going to be completed in a semester. They frequently chose concepts that would take multiple years to complete even for a team of full-time veterans. As students divided up the work for these oversized projects, practically no one was able to complete their assigned portion, and assembling a bunch of incomplete parts frequently resulted in a whole project that felt even more incomplete.

Additionally, for big projects that take a whole semester to complete, accountability is a huge issue. Invariably, students would tell their teachers and teammates that their portion of the project was coming together nicely, but when it came down to the wire, "all of the sudden" they would start to experience setbacks. In reality, they hadn't been working at the pace their previous updates would have led you to believe.

And while you might expect that passion projects would have a strong enough allure to maintain student commitment after the semester was over, in reality, graduations, new projects, day jobs, class loads, and other factors all contributed to making it extremely rare for teams to stay together on a project across semesters.

In the end, far too many student projects went to the graveyard, never reaching a state that students felt confident putting them in their portfolio. But we were able to implement a project management solution that tackled many of these issues and resulted in a lot more complete projects. Again, can you guess what it is?

2

Why Is Scrum the Solution?

Like all magnificent things, it's very simple.

Natalie Babbitt, *Tuck Everlasting*

Chapter in a Tweet

Scrum may not be the most *efficient* way to handle a project, but it does ensure the **highest ROI** for complex projects.

CUSTOMERS AND COSTS

Throughout this book, I make reference to customers (or clients) and costs. Depending on your journey through life up to this point, you may not have worked on a project where money has been exchanged, which is typically a vital occurrence for defining who a customer is and what their costs are.

But discussions of costs and clients can be just as relevant to you as to someone in a professional setting. You just need to quickly make two conversions in your mind every time you see those words.

If no one is shelling out the dough, then the customer is the person who defines the project. If your professor gives you a final project and has very specific deliverables, then your professor is the client. Alternatively, if your professor gives you a final project that is substantially open to interpretation and customization, then you are the customer, even though the professor assigned the work.

If you are working on a passion project all by yourself, then you are the client. If you invite some friends to work with you, then you are their client, too. If another student persuades you to work on her project, then she is your client.

As for costs, you've heard the phrase that time is money. The time you and others spend on the project is definitely a cost. For many people, thinking about costs in terms of time is intuitive and gets the job done. Later in this book, we'll also talk about other ways to measure time and effort.

Review of Project Management Problems

Let's break out some of the different problems you'll face when working on complex projects.

1. Inaccurate estimations at project commencement
2. Poor work being done by inexperienced people
3. Losing enthusiasm for projects that take a long time
4. Clients want costly changes for free
5. Separate pieces of a project not working together well when it comes time to combine them
6. External circumstances severely hampering a project
7. Completed projects not resonating with customers

Certainly, more things could go on this list. It could probably be an entire chapter if not a book unto itself.

Non-Scrum Ways of Solving These Problems

These problems have been around for as long as projects have been around. Scrum is relatively young. So it goes without saying that many other solutions have been applied to these problems. Let's look at those.

Detailed Upfront Planning and Estimation

Many project management texts recommend that 5%–10% of a project's overall budget should be spent on upfront planning. The idea is that doing this upfront planning will help you anticipate and overcome roadblocks before they even happen. It'll help you staff the project properly. It allows the team and the client to get on the same page. It'll allow you to create contingency plans for parts of the project that are less certain. Certainly, a big upfront planning phase does give the team and a much clearer idea of what they are working on and how they can avoid many pitfalls.

Unfortunately, in the experience of nearly all project managers, you just can't anticipate *everything* that can go wrong. And you know what they say about things that can go wrong.

> Oh what I wouldn't do for the gift of prophecy!

Tight Employee Supervision and Hierarchies

Responding to the need to mentor inexperienced team members and catch small problems before they become huge issues, many teams have quite the hierarchy of professionals. When you're first hired, you may actually have the word "junior" in your title, then associate, then senior, then lead, then director, and so on, or some similar tiered system. This system certainly does telegraph what you can expect from a given individual, and it sometimes makes it clear who is supposed to mentor whom.

It also creates both real and perceived communication issues. Are you an associate graphic artist having trouble integrating your work with a senior programmer? Then tell your lead graphic artist, who will tell the lead programmer, who will talk to the senior programmer. It's inefficient and runs the added risk of creating misunderstandings and hurt feelings.

> Why did you tell my boss that my work sucks?!
> I didn't say your work sucks. I said your work is vacuous.

Team-Building Activities

How do you keep team members motivated on a long project? Take them bowling and buy them beer!

Bowling, beer, and their kindred activities and spirits are surely awesome, but the next day when people have to work on a project that is dragging is just a bummer that is bound to burn people out sooner or later; usually sooner. This holds true even if the leadership is positive and the environment is collegial.

> But please, don't take away my bowling and beer!

Detailed Contracts and Relationship Managers

Enough teams have gotten the short end of the stick when it comes to making changes that detailed contracts are commonplace. These contracts specify what is to happen if either party wants to, or accidentally, shake things up. There are even people whose job consists primarily of telling clients they can't have what they want, "per section 5e of the agreement." Having a good contract in place does help set expectations and quickly resolve disputes when they arise.

The problem is that the reason people want changes is almost always because they want to make it better. It doesn't feel good to work on a project that you know can be better, but that isn't going to be because there isn't any flexibility in the contract.

> I'm working on this project. It would be really cool, except that there's no budget to implement the best ideas. Awesome, right?

Complex Software for Managing Task Relationships and Dependencies

How do you solve problems you encounter making software? With software of course! In the case of project management, if Joe needs Sally's work to move forward, and Sally needs Tim's work for 5 days to do what she's doing for Joe, then you know that you're going to have a problem if Tim hasn't given his work to Sally at least 5 days before Joe needs it. Software can definitely help teams keep track of these relationships and catch little delays before the domino effect converts them to big delays.

Software solutions often struggle because they are only as good as the people that use them. If teams aren't regularly updating their progress, the tool becomes useless. Data being inaccurate is especially likely when you load in thousands of tasks, subtasks, dependencies, and due dates at the start of a project, many of which won't be relevant for months or even years.

Additionally, people lose motivation when they feel like they spend more time updating software than actually getting work done.

Focus Groups

How do you make sure your project doesn't fall flat when it launches? One way is to get people in a room and ask them how they feel about the idea. Focus groups definitely give you insight into how people think, how they might respond to a new product, what they'd be willing to pay, etc.

But such activities have a fatal flaw: what people say and what people actually do are often at odds with each other. They may say they wouldn't buy it, but when it comes out they do. Or they may say they'd pay $100 for it, but when it's released at $50, they don't buy.

If you can get people to put their money where their mouth is, you are way better off than just listening to their mouth.

Cost-Centric Project Management

It's worth taking a quick moment to talk about "why" companies have used the aforementioned approaches to solving their project problems. It's actually useful to bring back up the concept of return of investment (ROI). Here's the actual formula for ROI:

$$\text{Return on investment} = \frac{\text{Gain from investment} - \text{Cost of investment}}{\text{Cost of investment}}$$

If your algebraic brain hasn't been shelved for too long, you'll notice that one of the most obvious ways to increase ROI is to reduce the cost of the investment. Not surprisingly, many companies have put controlling costs first and foremost in their project management practices.

Additionally, when people make an investment of time or money, they frequently value predictability in their return. In fact, many people and companies value a predictable return over a higher return. As such, a large variety of project management practices are specifically designed to ensure that anything that would change the ROI of a project is avoided, even if the change has a decent chance of being in the positive direction.

The Waterfall

When you value predictability and low cost, your work starts to take a certain predictable life cycle:

1. Gather requirements
2. Design the solution
3. Implement the solution
4. Test and fix the solution
5. Release the solution

In such a project, the primary commandment is that once you have left a step, you do not go back. The inviolability of this commandment has led the industry to name this process the "waterfall," because just as a literal waterfall cannot flow up, you cannot go back to a previous step once you have moved on. The waterfall is often visualized as shown in Figure 2.1.

While the waterfall certainly has a decent track record for delivering the predictable returns it is designed to produce, it has a couple pitfalls. First, it is very unforgiving of mistakes and oversights made in previous phases.

FIGURE 2.1
The Waterfall Process.

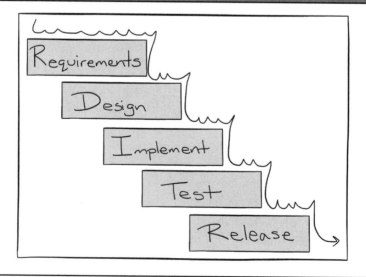

For example, if you get to the implementation phase and someone realizes that a key requirement was overlooked, there is a good chance you will keep going without the feature. In extreme cases, you may have to scrap the project and begin again in the requirements phase.

Second, the waterfall is not very good at integrating feedback from lower in the chain. For example, what if you get to the testing phase and one of your users has an amazing idea that would really improve the project? According to the waterfall, making that change would require additional work, which is an additional expense, which is assumed to lower ROI. There isn't a whole lot of consideration for how much the suggestion might increase the gain from the project and thereby more than make up for its costs.

Return on Investment Focus

I know you're tired of it but look one more time at the ROI formula:

$$\text{Return on investment} = \frac{\text{Gain from investment} - \text{Cost of investment}}{\text{Cost of investment}}$$

With a little more algebraic insight we recognize that, in addition to lowering costs, the other way to increase your ROI is to increase your gain. If great gains can be had for small costs, then your ROI can be improved in ways that aren't open to you if your mindset is focused only on keeping costs down.

Scrum encourages teams to determine the biggest gains their project has to offer for the lowest costs and to pursue them first. Conversely, it also encourages teams to leave out work that, while it may be "nice," isn't likely to produce big gains.

The Agile Manifesto

Having worked in companies that used the waterfall to solve project management challenges, and feeling like there must be a better way, a group of programmers at the turn of the century got together to concisely and artfully articulate their belief that things could be done differently. They called their consensus the *Manifesto for Agile Software Development*, which reads

We are uncovering better ways of developing software by doing it and helping others do it. Through this work, we have come to value

- *Individuals and interactions* over processes and tools
- *Working software* over comprehensive documentation
- *Customer collaboration* over contract negotiation
- *Responding to change* over following a plan

That is, while there is value in the items on the right, we value the items on the left more.

Scrum is an organized approach to achieving the objectives and priorities of the agile manifesto. Let's take a look at how scrum handles each of the agile values.

Individuals and Interactions

Scrum begins by defining three roles:

Product Owner—The product owner is responsible for determining what features of a project will generate the biggest gains. There can only be one product owner on a project.

Team Members—The team members are responsible for doing the actual work that is going to bring the product owner's vision to life. Most projects will have multiple team members who will likely have different skillsets.

ScrumMaster—The scrum master is responsible for making sure that team members are protected from unnecessary distractions. They also make sure that waterfall habits don't creep into the project.

Rather than providing very strict rules about how people are supposed to do their work, scrum instead provides a framework for making sure that the people in each of the three roles are communicating and cooperating for maximum effectiveness.

Working Software

Scrum doesn't want you to spend weeks or months planning your project, and months or years building your project before inviting people to use it. Instead, it encourages you to define an interval of no longer than 1 month during which you will assemble a working version of your project. After one interval is complete, the team begins a new interval interval immediately with the goal of building an even better version of the project, resulting in many working versions of your project throughout its life cycle. These intervals are called "sprints."

> **Sprint**—A fixed amount of time to make a working version of a project. Projects will go through many sprints during their lifetime, with each sprint improving upon the prior.

Customer Collaboration

Scrum has four ceremonies that take place during each sprint.

> **Ceremony**—A fancy word for the special meetings required by scrum. You can also just call them meetings if ceremony feels too highfalutin.

The four ceremonies are

1. Sprint planning
2. Daily stand-up
3. Sprint review
4. Sprint retrospective

We'll look at each of the ceremonies in depth later in the book. For the moment, just understand that the customer is invited to participate in all of the meetings, which ideally means daily contact.

Responding to Change

At the end of every sprint, everyone on the project gets to use something that works. Having the opportunity to use the thing you are building will probably change the product owner's feelings about which features are the highest priority. They may make the most important feature something that wasn't even on the radar before. Or they may increase the priority of something that was previously thought to be of low importance.

Scrum encourages teams to start their next sprint focused on the new priorities. Because of this openness to evolving priorities, scrum teams are generally discouraged from trying to plan many sprints ahead, because such long-term planning is likely to be frustrated by responding to change.

So Many Words, How About Some Pictures?

Behold, the scrum process visualized! (Figure 2.2).

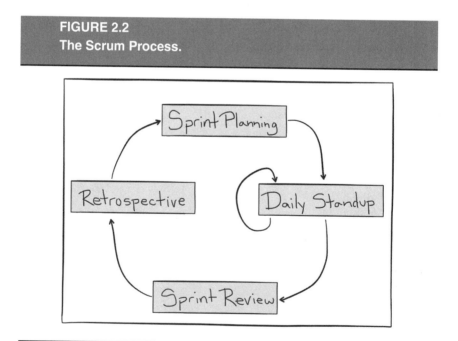

FIGURE 2.2
The Scrum Process.

FIGURE 2.3
Scrum Across Five Sprints.

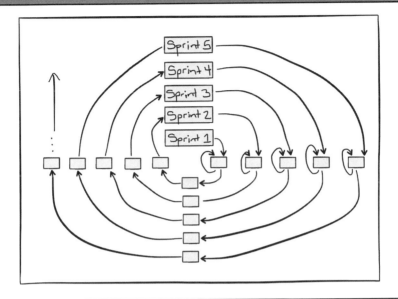

Want to see something that looks even cooler? This vortex of awesome is what a project that has been through five sprints might look like (Figure 2.3).

If you'd rather ride a waterfall than a whirlpool of excellence, then scrum isn't for you.

Is Scrum a Solution for Every Project?

Absolutely not! There are two primary cases where scrum is not a good fit.

The first situation is for projects that are simple. If you want to make a paper airplane, you don't need to name a product owner, ScrumMaster, and team members. Just make it! Additionally, sometimes there are big, long-term projects that are simple. For example, imagine that your long-lost, rich Aunt has a 120-acre undeveloped property. She says she'll write you into her will if you pick all the weeds on the property by hand. In this case, the project may take you several weeks, but the work itself is pretty simple and straightforward. In such a case, there is no need for sprint planning, daily stand-ups, etc. Just do the work!

The other scenario where scrum doesn't work well is for fixed-bid, fixed-timeline projects. In the opinion of agile practitioners, there isn't a good way to manage such projects, as they begin with a mythical expectation by definition. But if we set that notion aside for a second, when someone undertakes a project and there is a promise that certain things will be done at a certain time for a certain price, then scrum is not a fit. Such projects are not open to the change that scrum encourages. They may also benefit from a bit of micro-management to make sure they don't get off track, which is very antithetical to scrum values.

What Are the Alternatives to Scrum?

The waterfall isn't the only alternative to scrum. In fact, there are many other agile alternatives to the waterfall. Some of these include Lean, Kanban, and Extreme Programming. If you are interested in agile alternatives to scrum, the Internet and the library are your friends.

Why Is It Called Scrum?

Scrum is a term that comes from the sport of rugby. The cover of this book depicts a rugby scrum. There are at least three important metaphors for project management that can be taken from rugby, and from sports in general.

First, unlike American football, basketball, baseball, and many other sports, rugby is a game that is played continuously without interruption except in very specific cases, much like soccer. Contrast this to football where there is a built-in halt to the action after every single play. Scrum project management values keeping the action in a project going and therefore minimizing meetings, reports, and other things that stop people from actually working.

Second, as much as you value continuous action, things are going to happen that necessitate a reset. In the case of rugby, the ball may go out of bounds, or someone may throw it forward. When this happens, there is a specific way to resume the action, and that is the scrum. In scrum project management, the ceremonies, and in particular the daily stand-up, ensure that project teams are properly getting back to work after the action has stopped. In fact, the stand-up is sometimes simply called the scrum.

Finally, in sports, you inherently recognize the need to be flexible and respond to change. Teams may have a general strategy, such as double-teaming a particularly threatening player as often as possible, throwing a certain type of pitch, etc. However, you don't make detailed plans about how the game is going to unfold.

Can you imagine a team saying, "OK guys! Here's the plan. We're going to win the coin toss and choose to receive first. We're going to return the kick to the 30-yard line. For our first play we are gonna do a handoff, which will get us 7 yards. Then we'll do a short pass for 5 yards and a first down. Then… and finally, the last buzzer will sound and the final score will be 30–24. Ready? Break!" Such planning sounds absolutely ridiculous and is bound to fall apart within a couple plays, if not from the moment of the coin toss.

A waterfall lover might observe that a sporting contest involves an opponent who is actively trying to thwart you, whereas a project is an inanimate thing that has no interest in upsetting your plans. But experienced agile project managers will tell you that it will sometimes seem like your project is a far more formidable enemy than anyone you will encounter on the court or even the battlefield. If you believe that, then you are ready to begin your training, grasshopper.

3

Why ScrumButt

Do not take life too seriously. You will never get out of it alive.

Elbert Hubbard

Chapter in a Tweet

If you are inexperienced or separated from your team by long distances, you can't practice the purest form of scrum. But it can work!

Now that you understand the basics of scrum, it's important to note that it is actually an incredibly flexible project management framework. While it is most often associated with software development, it can also be used for things as diverse as moviemaking, marketing campaigns, or writing a book.

To practice scrum you need the following minimum requirements, which will be discussed in detail later:

1. People for each of the three scrum roles.
2. A defined sprint length.
3. A commitment from everyone on the team to attend the four ceremonies of scrum.

For each of the minimum requirements, scrum practitioners have established a wealth of best practices. Ultimately, this book is a collection of that knowledge, so it can't be completely summarized here. But just to give you an idea, here are a few:

1. Sprints should last 1–4 weeks, with the ideal length being 2 weeks.
2. The development team should be no more than seven people, with the ideal being three to five people.
3. Development team members should only be assigned to work on one project at a time.

And the list goes on. However, if you get together a room of people who *claim* to practice scrum, you are almost certain to hear someone say something like, "We use scrum, but we [do something totally inconsistent with scrum best practices/don't do something vital to scrum]."

Those of us who are passionate about scrum call this kind of implementation ScrumBut. What we really mean by ScrumBut is ScrumButt. In other words, typically such implementations fail completely or fail to unlock the full power of scrum.

When someone says

> We use scrum, but we don't do the sprint retrospectives.

The passionate scrum practitioner hears

> We use ScrumButt; we don't do the sprint retrospectives.

Understanding exactly why leaving out sprint retrospectives from your implementation of scrum is a bad thing requires understanding what a sprint retrospective is; knowledge of which I have yet to impart to you. But after reading this book you should get a good idea of all the different kinds of ScrumButt, and why many of them simply won't work.

If you're curious, other examples might include

> We use ScrumButt; we let 2 people share the role of product owner.
> We use ScrumButt; our sprint length is 3 months.
> We use ScrumButt; we don't require every sprint to end with a potentially shippable increment.

If you're going to bother doing scrum at all, you should aim to do it right. And to do it right, you're going to need to know what pure scrum is. This book will definitely teach you the principles and best practices of pure scrum.

I Sense That There's a ~~Butt~~ "But"

You would be right.

Successful implementations of scrum typically involve quitting your old project management system cold turkey. Organizations that try to adopt scrum in pieces almost always end up deciding that it doesn't work.

This happens because scrum is wholeness. It requires the synergy of its individual practices in order to realize its benefits. The individual practices by themselves sometimes don't work well and can even be counterproductive.

But in nearly every chapter of this book I've suggested steps for immediately applying scrum to your project. Depending on the rate at which you read and apply these changes, it's quite possible that you will be working on your project for many weeks having only applied a fraction of the changes described in the book.

The important thing to note is that during this transitional phase, do not deceive yourself that you are practicing scrum or even an acceptable version of ScrumButt. You won't be able to say that until you have finished the entire book and applied everything it has to offer. Before then, you can accurately say you're practicing ScrumButt, but the stench will probably be apparent to you and everyone around you.

I wish this was the only obstacle to adopting scrum with this book as your guide, but there are two perils that are even greater.

One of the best practices of scrum is that everyone on a project should work in the same physical space at the same time. The fancy word scrum practitioners use for this arrangement is *collocation*. But this book is largely intended for virtual teams.

Collocation—Placing people who work together on a project in the same physical space.

Another best practice of scrum is that development team members must be self-managing subject matter experts. But one of the primary audiences of this book is students, who are not yet likely to be experts in their field.

By definition then, if you work with your team virtually, or if you are a novice in your field, you can't practice pure scrum. If you're a newbie working virtually with your team, then the version of scrum you can practice is going to be seriously bastardized. Again, you are going to be practicing ScrumButt.

But whereas scrum purists might tell you to give up now because you are practically destined to fail, I am here to tell you otherwise. By knowing exactly what pure scrum is, and why it has the requirements and best practices it does, it is possible to alter these requirements and best practices while still achieving the same objectives and benefits.

Yes, ScrumButt is a formidable opponent. The battlefield of project management is strewn with the corpses of hundreds of teams that have tried to modify scrum and failed miserably. But it can be beaten! So pick up your slingshot, look the Goliath of ScrumButt in its stinking, proverbial eye, and quietly say to yourself between gritted teeth, "Let's do this."

4

How to Use This Book

If I had more time, I would have written a shorter letter.

Winston Churchill

Chapter in a Tweet

If you don't want to read the rest of this book straight through, then don't.

Now that you're hopefully convinced that scrum is an appealing way of managing projects, it's time to get a little more in depth about how this book is going to help you.

In Hamlet, one of Shakespeare's characters asserts, "Brevity is the soul of wit." By this yardstick, the principles of scrum are certainly a witty creation. It would be quite possible to satisfactorily explain scrum in a book much smaller than this one, and such a book (or, more likely, pamphlet) would be more valuable than the one you hold in your hand.

But ironically, you probably wouldn't buy it. To some degree at least, your perception of value for a technical text is correlated to how fat the text is. And, narcissistic though I may be, I didn't write this book simply to experience the genius of my own words. I want people to buy it and to use it! Therefore, I find myself compelled to provide enough content to meet your expectations of value.

However, as with other fine technical authors (yes, I'm going to include myself in that group), many of whom have written books far longer than the one you are now reading, I hope I am not wasting your time. It has been said

Repetitio Est Mater Studiorum | Repetition is the mother of learning

Latin Proverb

As it relates to this book, while I hope I have wittily explained scrum as concisely as can be done, I hope that the additional content is filled with activities, anecdotes, and observations that will serve to help you truly learn what scrum is and how it can be applied to your situation.

There's a principle from scrum that applies to how you read this book. One of the central tenets of scrum is that the worker needs to be empowered to work according to whatever workflow and style they consider best, not according to a workflow dictated by a boss or a company. In fact, scrum has very little to say about how to do whatever work will go into making a project a reality. Rather, it provides tools for ensuring that the most important work is getting done at any moment, and that a team of people with very different talents, styles, and responsibilities can coordinate their work as effectively as possible.

Similarly, while it pains me to compare the pleasure of reading this book to "work," or to compare myself as the author to your "boss," I think you need to read this book however you think you will get the most benefit out of it. Do not assume that because I am the author, I know what's best for you. For every person who picks up this book, there are probably that many "best" ways to read this book. I beg you to trust yourself and read this book the best way for you. I just hope that doesn't mean putting it down right now and never picking it up again!

In other words, if at any point you feel like you understand a principle, and my words seem to become unnecessarily repetitive, move on. Don't doubt yourself, do it! If you later find you think you missed something valuable, you can always come back.

That said, you should know that the ScrumButt NOW! breakouts are my favorite sections. They don't take particularly long to read or do, and I think these activities are highly valuable. I really hope you won't skip them! But these activities typically depend on you having a project that you are already working on or will begin shortly. If that doesn't apply to you, and you are reading this book purely as an informative exercise, ~~then I pity you~~ then you will probably not get much value out of these activities.

I think that about covers it. Unfortunately, if you have OCD learning tendencies like me, then you won't be able to bring yourself to skip a single word regardless of your situation. It is to you, my kindred spirit, that I most hope I have done a good job of being perfectly entertaining and informative.

Enjoy!

5

The First Secret of Scrum
The Product Owner

A committee is a group of people who individually can do nothing, but who, as a group, can meet and decide that nothing can be done.

Fred Allen

Chapter in a Tweet

Having one person who is responsible for the direction of the project simplifies everything.

We've established that scrum is built around the value of getting the greatest gains from a project at the lowest cost. Most complex projects offer their users multiple gains, so who decides which gains are the greatest? The product owner.

Let's imagine a fairly simple project (so simple in fact that you probably wouldn't approach it with scrum in real life, but don't let that keep you from learning). A wealthy executive moves into a new mansion. The executive frequently entertains business partners in her home and in fact will be entertaining an important guest exactly 1 week after she moves in.

The grounds have not been maintained in many months, and the executive wants the yard to be as impressive as possible for her first guest. The grounds have the following features (Figure 5.1):

1. Large flowerbeds all along the driveway
2. 12 trees in the front yard
3. A 5-acre lawn in the back

FIGURE 5.1
The Mansion Grounds.

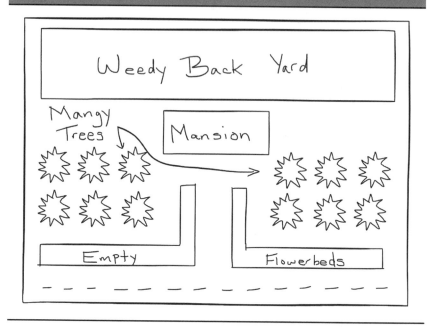

Currently, the flowerbed has only dirt, the trees are overgrown, and the lawn in the back is full of weeds. With current gardening staff, trimming the trees, pulling the weeds, or planting flowers will all take exactly 1 week each. It is not feasible to hire additional staff, so someone must decide which of the three features to improve for the arrival of the executive's first guest, while two must be left in their current state.

So who is the product owner? There are actually a few possibilities. I suggest that the executive herself is probably the best product owner for the scenario described. Given that she lives in the home, she is probably available frequently enough to answer questions for the garden staff (e.g., what kind of flowers should they plant). She is also likely to understand which features are most likely to be impressive to her guest.

Alternatively, suppose that the executive will be traveling on business during the week in question, and therefore won't be able to answer the staff's questions. Additionally, while she knows that beautiful grounds will impress her guests, she does not consider herself knowledgeable enough to decide between all the options. In such a case, the head gardener might make a suitable product owner.

If the executive is married or has a partner of some sort, perhaps he would make a good product owner.

Finally, consider that the person who the executive is trying to please is the guest. Additionally, the executive knows that landscaping is a passion of her guest's and that the guest would actually enjoy participating frequently in the project. In this case, the guest might be named as the product owner.

What Makes a Bad Product Owner?

Everyone enjoys being negative every now and then; so let's examine the role of product owner from a glass half-empty perspective.

Multiple Personalities

The product owner definitely needs to be one person with clear vision. The role of product owner absolutely cannot fall on multiple shoulders.

In our example, imagine that the executive and her husband are trying to share the role of product owner. They each want the flowerbed to be one solid color, but they disagree as to which color it should be. Or maybe one of them wants to plant flowers that will last for a very long time, while the other likes the idea of planting seasonal flowers and redoing the flower bed often.

Most projects have multiple people who care about the outcome. Therefore, the person named as product owner needs to synthesize these inputs, make decisions, and preemptively communicate with people who won't be getting their way. This is the primary talent of the product owner, and it's not easy!

Additionally, the individual who is chosen must be reasonably consistent. While scrum values changing directions as desirable when beginning a new sprint, the product owner must be consistent with their direction during each individual sprint. Product owners who change priorities in the middle of a sprint, or who give clear direction but later deny giving it, are definitely going to cause problems.

If team members have to navigate conflicting inputs from one or more people, someone is going to end up unhappy, and it's usually everyone.

Maybe you've had that professor who said, "I don't care about formatting just content." Then you get your paper back and you've had points taken away for using single spacing, not using APA citations, etc. This is an example of product owner with multiple personalities.

A TALE OF TWO PRODUCT OWNERS

One time, I took over a class for another professor who had an emergency that made her class load unmanageable. I knew she cared about the class I was taking over. In an effort to be nice, I told her that she could attend the class and offer feedback as often as she wanted.

In class, we were working on a game. Personally, I felt that the top priority was to make the game fun. The prior professor felt that the top priority was to include certain features that had been promised to the school board when the class was approved. Unfortunately, she and I didn't realize this difference of opinion, and therefore we didn't discuss it.

What neither of us knew was happening is that students would approach both of us separately to find out what they should be working on. Given our different priorities, we would invariably give them different directions. The students were then left to negotiate delivering on what I'd said or what the other professor had said.

Every time we reviewed progress, I was consistently disappointed that the students had worked on things that I didn't think were very valuable and hadn't worked on things that I thought were very important. The other professor felt the same way. Work was getting done, but we had a bunch of different features half done, instead of a few features done well. In short, the project suffered because there were two product owners setting conflicting priorities, and we never realized it and fixed it.

Indecisive

The product owner needs to have a clear vision about which features of the project are the most important. When two features are approximately equal in value, the product owner needs to quickly choose one of them to take priority over the other and move on.

Some people feel intimidated by the idea of declaring resolutely that one feature is more important than another. They're the sort of people who think every feature should get a participation ribbon, with no ribbons for first, second, and so on. These people make bad product owners because they may paralyze the whole project with indecision.

Unavailable

Even though every sprint begins with a planning session, there are still questions that will come up during the sprint that require the input of the product owner. If the product owner isn't timely in getting feedback to their team, then the team either won't be able to make progress or runs the risk of making the wrong decision and producing something that displeases the product owner.

In our example, maybe during the planning session, the product owner wants to tackle the flowerbed and use marigolds and tulips. During the sprint when the team goes to buy flowers, they find out that a virus has nearly destroyed the marigold population such that no marigolds are for sale. The product owner needs to immediately decide how to handle the situation.

Irresponsible

By this, I don't mean untrustworthy, but rather an unwillingness to accept responsibility. Going back to our example, imagine that the executive takes on the role of product owner and that she decides to focus first on a red, white, and blue flowerbed. The gardening team then executes her vision exactly as she described it.

When her guest shows up, he remarks that he thinks the flowers are tacky. A bad product owner will blame the gardening team for the ugly flowerbed. A good product owner will listen to the feedback, praise the gardening team for standing by her initial vision, and either stand up for her decision or implement changes based on the feedback in the next sprint.

Unintuitive

A project's reception depends on the degree to which the product owner was in tune with the target audience. A frequent mistake of product owners is to prioritize according to their personal preferences, rather than the needs of their market. Projects with such product owners are prioritizing the wrong gains, and their projects may struggle to make a decent ROI.

Unrespectable

I'm not talking about a person's moral character. I'm talking about the team's perception that the product owner is truly empowered to make decision about which features are the most important. There are a few different scenarios when the product owner won't be respected as the authority on feature priority.

1. The management of a company appoints a product owner that the team doesn't respect. This is particularly likely to happen in merger and acquisition situations, or when there is some kind of management shake-up, and the person who was the product owner or leader on a project is moved or demoted and a new product owner is inserted.
2. The person who should be the product owner doesn't have the availability to successfully fulfill the role, so a lackey is appointed in their place. But the lackey isn't successful at relating the vision of the should-be product owner. When the should-be product owner periodically reviews progress, she expresses dissatisfaction and expects the team to undo a lot of work that has been done at the direction of the lackey product owner.

THE WRONG PRODUCT OWNER

One of the initiatives I had at UAT was to integrate our graduate students with our undergraduates. I had a project-oriented class that I thought was an ideal opportunity to further that goal. The project we were working on was a passion project that one of our sophomore students had started. When we accepted his project, we told him that he would probably have to give up some of the leadership on the project in order to make the project work for the class, which included juniors and seniors, in addition to the aforementioned graduate students. He agreed to this requirement.

The founding student, who was pursuing a game art degree, was assigned a lead art role. A graduate student was assigned to be the product owner. The graduate student did an admirable job of prioritizing game features. However, the inexperienced sophomore student, though well intentioned, thwarted the graduate student's hard work.

During sprints, the founding student would focus on whatever he wanted. For example, the graduate student may have prioritized finishing the assets for the first level, but the founding student would put his effort into mocking up and modeling characters that wouldn't be necessary until the fourth level or beyond.

Because the founding student was so charismatic, and also because students felt an allegiance to him as the creator of the project, many students would flock to help him in whatever he worked on and would neglect their commitments to work on the priorities as determined by the product owner.

In the end, the project didn't make consistent progress on either the founding student's priorities or the grad student's. Not surprisingly, neither of them was satisfied with their role. What we should have done was either train the sophomore to be a good product owner or select a different project that was proposed by a graduate student.

Technically Minded

The product owner is supposed to advocate for the most valuable features of the project. Sometimes, understanding what needs to happen at a technical level to bring a project to life leads product owners to compromise their priorities based on what they think needs to happen workwise.

In the next chapter, we'll discuss how the product owner sets priorities in greater depth, but here's an example of a good priority the product owner might set if she were working to create a social media site:

- Users want to be able to update their status.

Notice that you don't need to be technical to understand that priority. Here's an example of a bad priority as it relates to a social media site:

- Create a database for user statuses

This priority betrays the fact that the product owner knows a little bit about how user statuses will be stored. By itself that wouldn't be a problem. The problem becomes apparent when you fulfill the priority of creating a database only to realize that the user can't actually create a status without additional work, such as exposing the database to the user through a front end.

Remember that scrum requires finishing a usable version of the project every sprint. The plain language priority makes that more likely to happen. Good product owners keep things in nontechnical terms, regardless of their own technical knowledge.

Bossy

Again, product owners are advocates for getting the most out of a project by working on its most important features first. She does not assign work to the team members. Later on, we'll discuss how to convert a product owner's priorities into tasks for the team but believe me when I tell you that the product owner isn't in charge of doing it for reasons that will become apparent. Product owners who try will ruin the scrum experience for themselves and their teams.

ScrumButt Modifications

Having a product owner is the first secret of scrum, and, as such, it is one you should not alter. There is no attribute of the product owner that is inherently adverse to student teams or teams that are working virtually. There is no reason you need more than one product owner. There is no reason you will benefit from having a technical product owner, etc.

That said, a new product owner, particularly one who is new to scrum, may have trouble getting used to the role. If she comes from a project management background, she may want to assign work. If she is technical, she may prioritize tasks instead of features. Like anything in life, she'll get better the more she does it. It is the job of the ScrumMaster specifically to make sure that the product owner doesn't break any scrum rules as she fulfills her role. A good product owner will also be open to feedback from other sources about how she can improve.

The Bottom Line

A great product owner sets clear priorities for the project and takes responsibility for the value the project delivers.

ScrumButt Thinking

1. Based on what you know about the product owner's role, can you think of other desirable traits for her to have? How about additional negative traits?
2. In the gardening example, in what order would you have prioritized the flowerbed, trees, and back yard. Why?
3. Can you think of a different way to divide the yard work for even greater effect on the first guest (e.g., half of one task and half of another)?

ScrumButt NOW!

1. Open the ScrumButt resources workbook.
2. Find the ScrumButt team members worksheet.
3. Put the name of the product owner in the appropriate space.
4. Give yourself a high five!

6

The Second Secret of Scrum
The Product Backlog

> The key is not to prioritize what's on your schedule, but to schedule your priorities.
>
> **Stephen Covey**

Chapter in a Tweet

The product backlog is a list of project features sorted by perceived priority to users. It's easy to understand but difficult to master.

When a team undertakes a brand new project, there are all kinds of information floating around about what the project will look like when it's done. Consider the basic feature list of a project like HealthCare.gov on day 1, in no particular order.

1. Browse insurance plans.
2. Join an e-mail list to receive updates about the site.
3. Pay for insurance plans.
4. Read about why insurance is important.

Recall that in waterfall project management, this list would be considered unchangeable. The object of the team would be to build the things on the list, nothing more or less, as quickly and inexpensively as possible. The waterfall frequently demands that a project be completed by a certain date, which ensures that costs are contained and that efficiency is prioritized.

Waterfall project managers typically think of progressing on the project in one of two ways. One option is to build it in chronological order according to the anticipated user experience. In this case, the first thing the team would work on would be the home page. When that's complete they move to the account creation page, etc. This approach has the advantage of allowing the testing of features as they become complete. On the other hand, many of the most important features don't come until the end of the experience, so you'll have to wait a long time to try those out.

The other waterfall option is to work on the project like a jigsaw puzzle. Different teams simultaneously work on the homepage, the account creation page, the plan browsing pages, the purchase pages, etc. This approach has the advantage of allowing people with different specialties to work independently. Conversely, when the different teams wrap up their work, which is frequently months or years after getting started, often the pieces don't fit together well.

Regardless of the approach, the managers in a waterfall project will break down *all* the items on the feature list into smaller and smaller increments, until finally every feature is broken down in bite-sized chunks, which will then be assigned to the team by the project manager.

In the case of HealthCare.gov, the opening day was set years in advance, so the team working on the project had multiple years to chew through their bite-sized task list. But when the curtain went up, the site wasn't working well. People experienced long delays or couldn't get on at all. There was a lot of disappointment and criticism. Such launches are all too common in the world of waterfall project management.

Hindsight is 20/20 as they say, so let's indulge in a little perfect vision. Could scrum have changed the launch of HealthCare.gov for the better? I think so, and it begins with the "product backlog," the first "artifact" of scrum.

Product Backlog—A flexible list of desired product features that is altered and prioritized by the product owner on a consistent basis.

Artifact—In scrum, an artifact is a tool that is used in the project management process. Ceremonies frequently revolve around team members creating and updating the artifacts.

The backlog begins just like the waterfall with a list of features, but the first thing that is going to happen is that the *product owner* is going to prioritize the list. It's important that the list be organized by the product owner and not delegated to someone else. Other people can give their input to the product owner about what they think is important, but the product owner ultimately determines where things fall.

The feature list should be prioritized according to what features are most important to users. As we discussed in the previous chapter, at this point it's very important to *not* think technically. Why? Thinking technically causes a product owner to think about workflow, capacity, dependencies, etc. To realize the advantages of scrum, the product owner needs to leave these concerns to other people, and only think about value.

In the case of HealthCare.gov, the product owner may have sorted the features like so:

1. Pay for an insurance plan.
2. Browse insurance plans.
3. Read about why insurance is important.
4. Join an e-mail list to receive updates about the site.

What's Not on the List?

You'll notice that there's no item saying, "log into the site." Surely, you say, logging in must be part of paying for an insurance plan, if not some of the other features on the list. That may be, but logging in is not a feature that users find *inherently valuable*. Have you ever said to yourself, "Gee, I wish there was another website I could log into!" Probably not, because logging in isn't something you care about. What you care about is seeing pictures of your friends, listening to music you like, seeing your calendar, etc. Logging in is something that many site developers need you to do in order to identify you, retrieve your information, etc.

When building and maintaining the product backlog, the product owner should be thinking about value and nothing else. Later on in the process, the scrum team will help the product owner know if things such as logging in, security certificate, database tables, and other things are required in order to bring a feature to life.

If knowledge were a nail and this book a hammer, this is a point I would pound into your head over and over.

Release Early, Release Often

Scrum teams work on the project features according to their priority. They specifically don't work according to the chronological experience of the entire product backlog. They especially don't divide up all the features in the backlog and work on them simultaneously. They choose the highest priority feature, and work to complete it first, before moving on to the next feature. But this isn't just a different way of dicing up the work that ends up with the same result. It is a completely different way of pursuing the work *and* releasing the value created to the target audience.

In the case of our example, the product owner has determined that users will get the most value if they can buy one affordable insurance plan online. Sure, having choices is good. Sure, educating the consumer is good. But, in the eyes of this product owner, those things are subordinate to making it so that users can buy one good plan. In this case, the scrum team would focus on giving users the ability to buy a single plan in as short a development time as possible. They would specifically ignore the fact that they will eventually need the infrastructure to host multiple plans. They would ignore the fact that they eventually intend to create an educational portal. They would focus exclusively on the thing the user values most, as determined by the product owner.

In scrum, when the team has reached the milestone of having built the most important feature, they don't just move on to the next feature in the list. Rather, they release the current version to their target audience, so that their users can immediately benefit from the value that the team has created. This also creates an opportunity for real users to give real feedback based on actual use of the project.

The members of great scrum teams eventually become feedback whores. It can be intimidating to release a project that is far from reaching the final vision the team has. You might fear negative reviews. You might worry about more work being put on your plate by demanding users. But once you've had the experience of getting feedback from real users within a few weeks of building a feature, you will get addicted. You will thrive on fixing your users' problems and improving their experience. You will take great satisfaction in giving users value as soon as possible, sometimes years sooner than if you wait for the entire project to be complete.

Grooming the Product Backlog

As the team gets more experience in the project, and as user feedback starts to come in, the product owner will want to make changes to the product backlog. Scrum encourages this, because so long as the product owner is focused on delivering the greatest value, changing priorities means making a product that will be more valuable to the target audience based on improved information. Again, whereas other project management systems are focused on building a predetermined feature list as inexpensively as possible, scrum is focused on giving users the most value as fast as possible.

One form of modification the product owner may make is adding new features. Going back to our HealthCare.gov example, imagine that the team first built a version of the software that let users buy one insurance plan and pay their premiums with Visa and MasterCard. After launching the product, the team gets a lot of feedback that users want to be able to use PayPal. The product owner may determine that adding this payment method, something that wasn't even considered earlier, is actually more important than adding the ability to browse more plans. In that case, the product backlog may be updated to read as follows:

1. Pay for an insurance plan using PayPal.
2. Browse insurance plans.
3. Read about why insurance is important.
4. Join an e-mail list to receive updates about the site.

Alternatively, suppose that users give feedback about PayPal but also express even greater interest about joining a list to be informed when new plans are released. Going one step further, imagine that the product owner has received data that suggest that people who end up at HealthCare.gov are already convinced of the need for health insurance, and therefore education about the importance of insurance is a low-value feature that's not even worth building. With all this in mind, the product owner might groom the backlog like so

1. Join an e-mail list to receive updates about the site.
2. Pay for an insurance plan using PayPal.
3. Browse insurance plans.

This team has the satisfaction of giving users value early in the development process, and the project they are building is changing from the original vision, becoming more of what users actually want (Figure 6.1).

AsABIWaB

Thus far in our example of HealthCare.gov, we've only talked about what the consumer wants. But most projects have many stakeholders. In our example, other stakeholders might include insurance companies, politicians, the press, site administrators, and more.

Adding in some of those concerns, a product backlog might look something like

1. Track how many people visit the site.
2. Enter insurance plan details.
3. Join an e-mail list to receive updates about the site.
4. Pay for an insurance plan using PayPal.
5. Browse insurance plans.

As the product backlog starts to grow, it can be hard for the product owner to remember why features are important and therefore prioritize them properly. It can also be tempting to add tasks to the product backlog instead of features. One thing that can help the product owner make these choices is to include the audience as part of the feature description. One standardized method that was originally developed by scrum expert Mike Cohn is the "As a *blank* I want *blank* so that *blank*" naming convention, or AsABIWaB (uh-SOB-ee-wob) for short. (Yeah, we left off the SoThaB, but those extra syllables are a real buzzkill.) Let's dissect this way of describing our features.

As a Blank

Fill in the blank with the audience that wants the feature. This part of the phrase reminds the product owner and the rest of the team who stands to benefit by the implementation of the feature, which can be an important factor in determining how important something is.

FIGURE 6.1
The Unexpected Path.

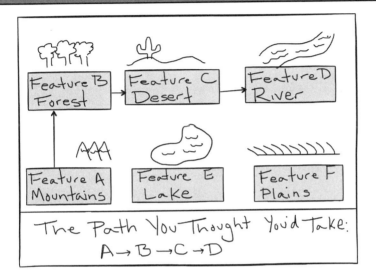

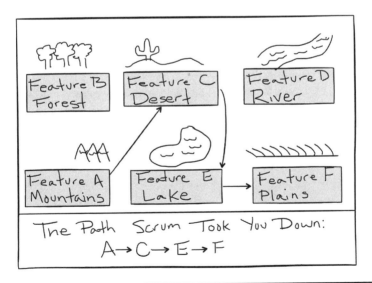

I Want Blank

Fill in the blank with a short description of the feature; pretty straightforward.

So That Blank

Fill in the blank with a short description of why this feature is important to the audience that desires it. This can be very helpful in distinguishing between features that are nice to have and features that are essential to the value proposition the project hopes to offer.

Back to Our Example

Let's apply this to our example backlog:

1. As a politician, I want to know how many people visit the site so that I can attack my political opponents.
2. As a consumer, I want to join an e-mail list to receive updates about the site so that I can come back when there are more plans to choose from.
3. As a consumer, I want to pay for an insurance plan using PayPal so that I don't have to type my credit card info.
4. As a consumer, I want to browse insurance plans so that I can make sure I'm choosing the best one for my situation.
5. As an insurance company, I want to make my plan available for purchase so that I can profit from universal health care.

When we phrase our features in this way, we call them user stories. You want your product backlog to be filled with stories, not just features. Good stories, in scrum as in literature, have a pretty good chance of being understood by a child as well as a grandma.

User Story—A description of a project feature written from the perspective of the target audience.

That's Not a Story!

At some point, a product owner may feel like getting lazy. This is particularly true of product owners with some technical ability, who might try to add something like this to the backlog:

> Use JavaScript to verify password strength.

This is a bad item for the product backlog. A nontechnical user can't understand it. Even for someone who understands what it means, it's hard to tell if it's a complete feature or if it's a task. When you stick to AsABIWaB, you'll get something like

> As a consumer, when I create an account I want to know if my password meets the site requirements before I submit my information, so that I don't have to retype and resubmit my information if it isn't.

In most projects, the target audience will never see your product backlog, and neither will your grandma. If everyone on a project understands the first story, is it really that big a deal to rewrite it? Yes, and here's why. The first story isn't really a story at all; it's an incomplete feature; a task. To explain this particular example, I've got to get especially boring for a few sentences. The code that verifies if a password meets the requirements is not the same as the user interface that tells consumers if the password has passed or not. In other words, it would be possible to use JavaScript to verify a password, but the consumer still have no idea whether or not that verification passed. The second story makes sure that the team considers the whole process involved in bringing the users' desires to life.

Another bad story might look like

> As a consumer, I want Healthcare.gov to be awesome, so that I love using it.

Even though this story is phrased using AsABIWaB, it doesn't really convey any useful information. What is the definition of awesome? What goes into making a site awesome? This story raises more questions than it answers and can't really be broken down into tasks.

In the case of both of these bad examples, it's not the end of the world if either of these stories ends up on the product backlog, because the backlog is a living document. If a bad story makes it onto the list, it won't be long until the team figures out that it needs to be modified and will work with the product owner to do just that.

The Devil Is in the Details

One of the mantras of scrum is that stories represent a conversation. The product backlog is not intended to be comprehensive documentation of every feature of a project. Rather, it is a high-level overview of the project, and it is understood that team members will need to discuss exactly what each story means, and what will need to be done to consider the story completed.

Later on, we'll talk about how we take features out of the product backlog to work on during a sprint. As you might imagine, some features are so big that they can't be completed in a single sprint so they need to be broken down. On the other hand, in order to remain flexible and not to waste time, scrum doesn't want you to break down features that won't be worked on for a very long time. For now, just remember that the product backlog should be comprised of complete features that would make sense to a user. Err on the side of not breaking things down, rather than breaking them down too much.

Where Does the Product Backlog Live?

Even though scrum is frequently used to make virtual goods and services, scrum experts are huge fans of using index cards, cork boards, sticky notes, butcher paper, whiteboards, and other physical media to track resources and monitor project progress and tend to frown on software solutions.

This isn't just a strange quirk held by strange people who like strangely named project management systems. There are some good reasons for it.

The first reason is community. Having a physical dashboard creates opportunities for team members to look each other in the eye during meetings and also randomly throughout the day as they update the board. The spontaneous conversations that come out of this face time are frequently valuable for making a project better or getting work done faster.

The second reason is the speed of implementing change. If you decide you want a new dashboard in a software system, you have to design the user interface and program it. If you are using a third-party software, it may be

FIGURE 6.2
Example Product Backlog.

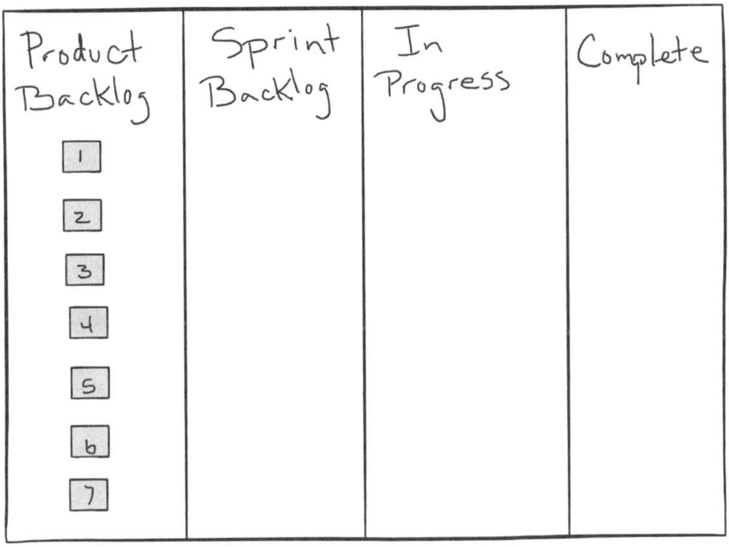

Product Backlog	Sprint Backlog	In Progress	Complete
1			
2			
3			
4			
5			
6			
7			

impossible to get a new dashboard, or you may have to wait for a long time until your vendor implements your feature request. If you decide you want to track something on a physical board, it's frequently as simple as grabbing a piece of paper and writing on it.

The third reason is that physical things are just fun, like collectible cards and pogs!

For many teams, the product backlog takes the form of sticky notes on a whiteboard. One reason for using sticky notes instead of just writing on the whiteboard is so that you don't have to erase and rewrite the tasks every time you change a priority, which gets particularly cumbersome if a whole series of stories needs to shift one direction or another (Figure 6.2).

Modifications for ScrumButt

The product backlog is at the heart of scrum. You definitely do not want to modify the principles of listing out the features that define your project and working on them in priority order.

This next point isn't really a modification, but rather a warning. If your product owner is inexperienced, he may have trouble creating a coherent feature list or prioritizing the list. The rest of the team, especially the ScrumMaster, should be prepared to be helpful without taking the role away from the product owner.

What virtual and student teams may need to modify is where the backlog lives. Virtual teams don't get together physically very often, if ever. Likewise, many student projects might not have a dedicated space where a physical backlog will be safe from janitors, other classmates, etc. With those constraints, physical versions of the product backlog are probably not ideal. I recommend using an online spreadsheet to keep track of the product backlog.

Another thing young scrum teams struggle with is how to phrase stories. AsABIWaB is a tool to help the team, especially the product owner, understand the importance of features and what will be required to implement them. It also helps the team communicate with stakeholders who aren't technical and/or aren't typically present at the ceremonies. However, I've seen some team members get really hung up on the phrasing. They know something needs to get done, but they can't think of how to phrase it AsABIWaB style. This leads to them feeling that scrum is preventing them from quickly getting work done. If this frustration starts creeping up with some members of your team, it's OK to temporarily sacrifice perfect format and allow poorly phrased stories in exchange for team morale and productivity. When things are a little smoother, you can see if the team members who struggled are ready to try AsABIWaB again.

Finally, I'd caution you against diving into specialized project management software for your first few projects, including solutions that tout scrum compatibility. Once you feel comfortable with scrum, these programs can make a lot of activities easier, but trying to learn scrum and learn scrum software simultaneously is probably biting off more than you can chew and will likely leave a sour taste in your mouth.

The Bottom Line

By keeping your eye focused on the value of complete features and working on the most valuable features first, your team will have a successful project and a satisfying experience bringing it to life!

ScrumButt Thinking

1. If you were the product owner for HealthCare.gov, what feature do you think would have been the most important?
2. Suppose a product owner for HealthCare.gov decided that browsing through plans was the most important feature, how would that have changed the development process?
3. What other features do you think would have been on the real product backlog for HealthCare.gov?

ScrumButt NOW!

1. Open the ScrumButt resources workbook.
2. Find the ScrumButt product backlog worksheet.
3. List all the features of the project.
4. Edit your feature list to conform to AsABIWaB style.
5. Have the product owner sort the list according to value to users.
6. Shake your ScrumButt for joy!

7

The Third Secret of Scrum
The Superheroes

Talent wins games, but teamwork and intelligence win championships.

Michael Jordan

Chapter in a Tweet

Treat your team like superheroes, not like children who need constant supervision.

OK. You've got a well-defined set of priorities that you want to turn into a working project. What's next? You assemble the superheroes that are actually going to make it a reality.

Different teams refer to the people who do the work by different names. Some people just call them team members. I happen to love that term because of the sports metaphor. However, in certain contexts it can be a little ambiguous, because the product owner and ScrumMaster are members of the scrum team, which can get confusing when trying to distinguish between those roles and the team members who specifically bring the project to life. Another term that is frequently thrown around is developer. In many contexts, a developer is a computer programmer, but on scrum teams the term is frequently used more generically to refer to anyone bringing the project to life, including artists and people with other nonprogramming talents.

Developer—Someone who works directly on a project to bring it to life. They can be from any discipline, not necessarily someone who codes. Affectionately known as superheroes.

But if you ask me, superhero is the most accurate and clear way of referring to the people who get their hands dirty bringing the product owner's vision to life. So let's run with that metaphor a little more as we discuss the characteristics of good developers.

Super Diverse

Have you ever heard about the team of superheroes who all have the same power? Me neither. Superhero teams are nearly always composed of people who have different talents and temperaments. This way, they're able to do way cooler things that require two or more different abilities. For people who enjoy comic books and movies featuring teams of heroes, a lot of the appeal is seeing the way in which the unique powers combine in order to create really cool effects.

Unfortunately, a lot of project management teams ignore the lessons of superhero team composition and decide to organize themselves by specialty. On these projects, all the graphic designers sit together, all the server programmers sit in a different place, and so on. In business-speak, these types of arrangements are called silos, and they are known to reduce cooperation and increase territorial behavior.

Silo—In business, a group of people, typically from one department, who are not accustomed to cooperating with employees of the same company outside their group.

The antidote to silos is to organize according to *cross-functional teams*. On these projects, all of the different people necessary to bring a feature together are organized into a single team. In the case of a video game, you might have a programmer, a game designer, a 2D artist, and a 3D artist all on one team. Because all of these team members have things they need to give to (and get from) each other, organizing this way facilitates clear communication, helps the team plan better, anticipate roadblocks, and navigate them together when they do arise.

> **Cross-functional Team**—A team that has members representing a wide variety of talents and specialties.

Super Leaders, Not Super Bosses

On a traditional project, there is frequently a hierarchy, with some people having titles such as director of design, lead designer, associate design manager, and so forth. People on these projects tend to focus on getting to the next level, which usually comes with more money, in addition to more prestige and responsibility.

Have you ever noticed that superhero teams almost never have a hierarchy, and sometimes forego a leader altogether? They view themselves as peers. When making plans, they seek buy-in from each other and are grateful (or at least accepting) when someone points out a flaw in the plan. Similarly, scrum teams frequently forego titles that indicate rank and prefer to see everyone on the team as an equal collaborator. In the business world, this kind of organization chart is called flat, as contrasted with the pyramid-shaped organization chart that tends to dominate many companies. Flat organizations are praised for being able to quickly implement innovation, and quickly respond to change, because there is less bureaucracy and red tape people have to go through to get things done. Because the goal of scrum is to maximize value vs. stick to the plan, these traits are highly prized.

Super Competent

When superheroes get into a fight, even if they have a leader, they don't sit around and wait for the leader to give them instructions. They all act independently with an eye toward the objective. They keep each other up to date and warn each other when there are unexpected problems that can adversely affect the rest of the team. They have each other's backs, and even though things rarely go exactly according to plan, they work out because each member of the team knows how to use their powers to maximize the objective.

Contrast that to how teams of villains usually work. The boss villain usually has a master plan. When things don't go according to the plan, the henchmen usually have no ideas how they can use their talents in order to save the situation and achieve the objective; that is, if they even know the objective.

In scrum, in order to perform at the level of a superhero team, you also need people who know what they're doing, who can work and make decisions without constant supervision. A person of this skill level is frequently referred to as *subject matter expert*, or SME. What you want to avoid is that quintessential storyline where a novice wants to tag along to the fight, the heroes say no because the novice will get in the way, the novice sneaks along anyway, fighting breaks out, and the novice actually does get in the way and nearly causes everything to fall apart. Fortunately, the heroes have the talent to save the overeager newbie and to win the confrontation.

Subject Matter Expert—A person who is recognized as an authority in their field.

Super Hideout

Superheroes usually all crash in the same place, and it's usually a pretty cool place. They've got the technology they need, the recreational space they need, places to plan together, places to be alone when necessary.

When working on a project, physically being together speeds up communication. Usually, it's pretty easy to say out loud, "what's this?" and physically point at your screen. Alternatively, opening up your e-mail and typing out your question, capturing and marking up screenshots, and wondering how long it will take someone to get back to you is a process that is sometimes lengthy and often causes great frustration.

For this reason, scrum teams typically reject the idea that the savings and convenience of working virtually outweigh the benefits of being in the same room as the people you work with. The fancy word for working together is colocation.

Colocation—The practice of having people who work with each other physically occupy the same space; typically the same room, not just the same building or campus.

Super Exclusive

Remember that superhero team the Fantastic 40? Of course you don't, because they don't exist. Superheroes tend to work in small groups that can usually be counted on the fingers of one hand, or two hands if it's a big group.

Scrum practitioners generally agree that the ideal size for a scrum team is 5, plus or minus 2. That number doesn't include the ScrumMaster and the product owner. The reason for valuing small groups so much has to do with communication. Because in scrum we treat everyone as a peer, we expect that everyone on a team will be communicating directly with each other, as opposed to communicating with a boss, who will then communicate with other people. Figures 7.1 and 7.2 illustrate how many more lines of communication a team of peers who communicate directly with each other have than a team that uses a boss to filter all communication.

In scrum, we believe that organizing as peers has big benefits for creativity and problem solving. But we also believe that these benefits start to be overshadowed by confusion and complexity when teams become large.

FIGURE 7.1
Lines of Communications in a Strict Hierarchy.

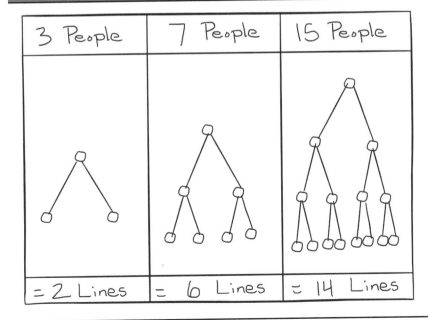

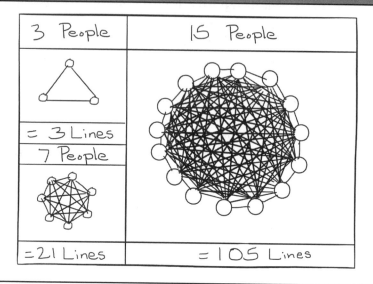

FIGURE 7.2
Lines of Communication between Peers.

Modifications for ScrumButt

Finally, we're getting into a portion of scrum where modification is actually necessary for student and virtual teams! But let's begin by looking at the things that we should not modify.

Small teams are really important for realizing the benefits of scrum. If you have a class of 20 students, I suggest making three to six teams and having each team work totally independent of each other.

A GIANT TEAM

One time I ran a special topics course that brought together students from multiple disciplines and experience levels (sophomores to seniors) who all wanted to work on one big game, a side-scrolling 3D brawler reminiscent of Double Dragon.

As a learning experience, it was incredible. I truly believe that class did more for the careers of the students who took it than any other class they could have taken at that time. The knowledge gained about group dynamics and accountability alone was deeply valuable, not to mention the technical knowledge.

However, many students didn't particularly enjoy the experience, and therefore I don't recommend it for general use. Even though we organized the students into multiple small teams, assembling the work of the small teams into a coherent whole was very cumbersome and was the ultimate source of the majority of student frustrations.

In future classes, we had small teams of students work on their own games, instead of on portions of one big game, and things went much smoother, leading to higher satisfaction.

If you are a virtual team, you may be working on your project after hours. What your core team lacks in time, do not try to make up for with bodies. If you make the team larger, in all likelihood your project will go slower, not faster, and it will be a messy Frankenstein that will be difficult to build on over time.

Next, you can't practice scrum without cross-functional teams; that can be difficult in a university setting, where a typical class is probably comprised exclusively of students with a particular set of skills, for example, all artists or all programmers. In such cases, there are two basic possibilities for implementing scrum. The option that I favor is for students to recruit team members from other disciplines outside the classroom. This provides the benefits of networking and also gets the students used to the needs and styles of other disciplines.

However, for a variety of reasons, such collaborations may not be possible in your case. I then recommend having students take on the other roles on a per sprint basis. Suppose a particular class is composed of programmers, but the midterm projects need teams of three programmers, a user interface designer, and a digital artist. Two of the programming students could play the roles of designer and artist for a sprint and then rotate with other students on their team for future sprints. It is understandable that the output of the students working outside of their discipline will be lower in quantity and quality, but they will gain a little experience that will help them empathize with people from outside their own discipline in the future.

For student teams in traditional school environments, colocation is usually pretty easy. For online students, colocation is more difficult. Virtual teams are, by definition, not collocated. I suggest two basic strategies for seizing the benefits of colocation in these scenarios.

First, could you change the way you work to allow for colocation? For example, imagine a team of hobbyists that live in the same town. They decide to work on a project together and each promises to dedicate 1 hour per weeknight, which they do from home. This group would likely see greater results if they were able to reorganize their work and get together for 5 hours over the weekend or 10 hours every other weekend.

Second, if you can't actually change the way you work in order to work together physically, take advantage of modern technology to create a virtual workspace that's as close to the real thing as possible. For example, if the group above hops on a Skype call or Google Hangout every night for an hour, then whenever someone has a question, they can just start talking and share their screen if necessary. The difference in inertia between already being in a call vs. firing up a call only when you encounter a problem is a big one that shouldn't be underestimated.

Finally, let's deal with the topic of expertise. Fortunately, it's typically just as easy to recruit SMEs to virtual teams as it is for collocated teams. However, students, by definition, are not experts. This problem can be tackled in a variety of ways.

One of my favorite suggestions is for students to recruit SMEs from industry to advise them. I have found that people are not only willing to help students in this way, but that they find it very satisfying. Depending on the scope and aspirations of the project, a professor may be able to fulfill this role.

Another thing student teams can do is simply allocate sprint time for each student to become an "expert" (or more likely, minimally conversant) in whatever issues are relevant to the highest ranked items in the product backlog.

Another thing you'll find is that people who are inexperienced do not want to be treated like peers; they want a boss or at least a clear leader. For this reason, it can be beneficial for teams that are new to scrum to establish a team hierarchy. However, if you go this route, remember that the ultimate goal is to make team members self-sufficient and to move them into a peer role as soon as possible.

The Bottom Line

Student and virtual teams struggle to have the attributes that are known to make for successful scrum teams. However, ScrumButt can be successful when these teams are very intentional about organizing in ways that address their weaknesses while striving to take advantage of as many best practices as possible.

ScrumButt Thinking

1. Would your team benefit by recruiting a subject matter expert in one or more areas? How can you attract such a person?
2. How can your team reorganize your work schedule and habits in a way that will allow you to get more of the benefits of colocation?

ScrumButt NOW!

1. Open the ScrumButt resources workbook.
2. Find the ScrumButt team worksheet.
3. List all the superheroes on the project.
4. Do a dance worthy of being called the ScrumButt!

8

The Fourth Secret of Scrum
Sprint Planning and Sprint Backlog

Being a good teammate is when you try to sprint down a ball that everyone thinks is going out of bounds. But you go after it anyways and you get it.

Mia Hamm

Chapter in a Tweet

To bring the product backlog to life, you pick the high-priority features, break them down, and get them done.

The Promise

Things are getting juicy! You've got a product owner and a prioritized list of the features that are going to make your project unique and successful. You've assembled a crack team and figured out how to maximize your ability to communicate and work together. Now it's time to put some points on the board by working fast and hard to make one or more features real.

A sprint is a promise made by the scrum team to the product owner. Specifically, it's a short-term promise about how much work is going to get done over the course of the next 1–4 weeks. If you make a promise, you better have a plan for keeping it.

Sprint planning is where the rubber meets the road, and it's one of the hardest things for scrum teams to master. There's an incredible art to getting enough detail and input to make accurate estimations possible, while not getting so bogged down in the details that people become frustrated and lose enthusiasm.

Now that we're talking about how much work is going to get done, we can attend to the part of project management that traditional project managers love so much: figuring out how much effort it's going to take to get stuff done. Finally!

Conversations

Each sprint is built around the "sprint log."

> **Sprint log**—A small portion of the product backlog that the team is going to implement during the next sprint.

One principle that helps teams get the right amount of information is to view items in the sprint log and product backlog as placeholders for conversations. Ultimately, the vision for the project lies in the head of the product owner. The expertise to make that happen is in the heads of the team members. The goal isn't to get out so much information that either of these people could be replaced, it's to make sure that enough conversations have been had that the person who has to do the work is empowered to do it, and for there to be a brief record of what those conversations entailed.

Capacity

The first step in taking things from the product backlog to the sprint log is to determine how much capacity you have in the sprint.

The first ingredient in your capacity is going to be the length of your sprint, which should be 1–4 weeks. The second ingredient in your sprint capacity is going to be the number of people on your team. The third factor is going to be the number of productive hours your team members can put in per sprint.

Spring length in weeks × Team size

× Productive hours per week per team member = Capacity in hours

On a full-time team, this equation might yield a number like 300 man-hours. However, there's one other ingredient that's important both for understanding what a team can do and understanding how teams improve over time, which is the productivity of each hour spent.

Two teams that work for the same amount of time on an identically scoped project are likely to work at different rates. In fact, the same team that works together for a year can probably do more with 300 hours than they could when they first started working together a year earlier. It's the nature of learning and getting better.

It would be OK if this improvement was just recognized generically. "Wow! We sure have come a long way in the last year. We get so much work done together." In fact, for teams new to scrum, I think that is probably the best way to handle it.

However, experienced scrum teams have a strategy for estimating their capacity that also allows them to measure their improvement over time, and I want to at least share it with you.

Back to Gardening

Let's revisit our gardening example from a few chapters back. Imagine that there are two flowerbeds to be planted. One is 20' × 20' and the other is 20' × 40' (twice the size of the first). Also imagine that there are two people who can plant them. One is a spritely young guy, who is working with the landscaping company to pay his way through college. The other is a friendly retiree, who enjoys gardening and figured it wouldn't hurt to earn some extra money while doing something he enjoys. The retiree can plant a flowerbed at about half the rate of the college student.

If we ask each of these people to estimate the jobs by hour, we would expect that the college student would predict that the jobs can be done in half the time of that predicted by the retiree. However, we would also expect that each of them would agree that the big flowerbed will take about twice as long as the small flowerbed.

If we "officially" estimate the task according to the college student's speed, but the retiree ends up doing the job, there's a good chance we won't allocate enough time to get it done. Conversely, if we use the retiree's estimate but the college kid does the work, he may stand around for a long time twiddling his thumbs after he finishes the job. We know one job is bigger than the other.

We also know that who actually does the job effects how much work we are going to be able to get into our sprint. How can we account for this?

Average Joe Hours

I've known some really talented people named Joe in my day. But the *average Joe* idiom is a powerful one, so I'm going to borrow it. One way to address the estimation problem is for the team to standardize estimates according to an average Joe. This person could be real or imagined. Maybe someone on your team is actually named Joe, or maybe you use the youngest person on your team, or maybe the most experienced. Alternatively, your Joe can be a fictitious person whose capability is easy enough for the team to imagine, such as a freshman, sophomore, junior, or senior, or maybe an imagined industry veteran.

To make use of this strategy, when teams estimate work for the purpose of building the sprint log, they don't think about how long it would take if they do the work themselves or the person who will actually end up doing the work. Instead they estimate how many hours it would take their average Joe to do.

One note, your average Joe should be assumed to have a similar skill level in all disciplines that your project requires. In other words, if your average Joe is a real person who is an artist. Don't assume that it will take the artist 3 weeks to program one working line of code, even if that is what would happen in real life.

Story Points

There's one more level of abstraction that has become the default in scrum. Instead of simply estimating hours according to the work rate of a particular, potentially fictitious person, we remove the reference to hours completely by creating a bank of example stories and estimating all tasks relative to the stories in the bank. The stories in the bank will be estimated in a point system we call… wait for it… story points. The actual effort required to complete a story point will differ for every team, and in fact every person on every team. But the whole point (pun intended) is that these variations between individuals and teams don't matter for the purpose of planning and estimating.

Story Points—A way of estimating the effort to complete a task that isn't based on the work rate of a particular person but rather on comparing the task to other tasks.

The first thing to do is figure out what one story point means to your team. For most teams new to agile, I've found that it makes sense for your first baseline task to be one that is relatively simple, maybe something that would take your average Joe a few hours to do. In the case of our gardening example, maybe planting a 10′ × 10′ flowerbed with daisies becomes one story point.

Now what we want to do is create a larger bank of examples that we can estimate relative to a 10′ × 10′ flowerbed. It wouldn't be incredibly useful to create a story point bank based on other size flowerbeds planted with daisies. The answer to that question is just one of multiplying. We also want to avoid getting too nitty-gritty about the details. The difference between 1 and 1.25 story points is not important to figure out. As a rule of thumb, many teams figure out the Fibonacci numbers: 1, 2, 3, 5, 8, 13, and 21. Other teams will use powers of 2: 1, 2, 4, 8, and 16.

At the landscape company, maybe a part of their story point bank looks like this

- 1 point—Plant a 10′×10′ bed of daisies
- 2 points—Mow a typical lawn (front and back)
- 4 points—Cut down a palm tree and haul away the stump
- 8 points—Hang Christmas lights.
- 16 points—Create a 3D landscape design concept for an average home.

Creating the story point bank is an important activity for a scrum team that is new to story points, even if the team is familiar with scrum. It should involve everyone, not just be the brain child of one key person on the team.

Going back to our example of two flowerbeds to be planted, one 20′ × 20′ and another 20′ × 40′, we can say that the first flowerbed is four story points (there are four 10′ × 10′ spaces in a 20′ × 20′ space) and the second is eight story points. It doesn't matter if the college kid does the work or the retiree does the work, the amount of story points is the same. Finally, if there were factors about these jobs that made it more or less complex than a typical flowerbed, we could adjust our estimate accordingly (Figure 8.1).

FIGURE 8.1
Man-hours vs. Story Points.

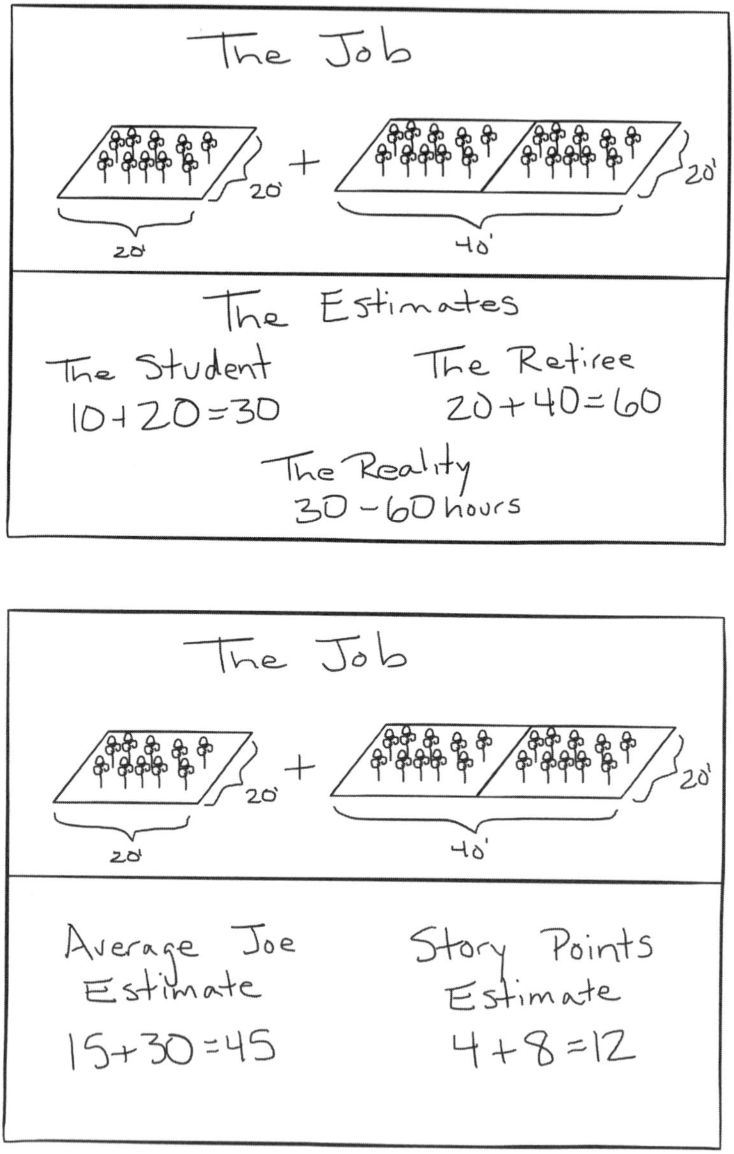

The Job

20' + 20'

20' 40'

The Estimates

The Student
10+20=30

The Retiree
20+40=60

The Reality
30 - 60 hours

The Job

20' + 20'

20' 40'

Average Joe
Estimate
15+30=45

Story Points
Estimate
4+8=12

Using Story Points to Determine Capacity

Let's say our landscaping team has five people. It would be a mistake to think that if the college student can do 10 story points per sprint, then our capacity is 50 story points. Similarly, it would be a mistake to assume that everyone has the same capacity as our retiree, or 25 story points. Our actual capacity is probably somewhere in between and depends on the specifics of our group. In fact, for a recently assembled team, I recommend setting the goal to hit about half your theoretical capacity in the first sprint.

How Much Work Should We Estimate?

You'll recall that traditional project managers want to estimate everything in the product backlog and use those estimates to predict how long the entire project will take. But because we're being agile, we know that the things at the bottom of the product backlog may never get worked on, because other features with a higher priority are constantly being placed above it. We also recognize that people are notoriously bad at being able to estimate very large tasks/projects, and that small errors will ripple out and become huge problems if the entire project is based on them.

Therefore, instead of estimating the whole product backlog, you'll begin by estimating at least enough features so that you have the capacity of one sprint broken down. It's also acceptable to estimate a second sprint in detail, but I wouldn't get too deep into features that are three or more sprints away, because their future is uncertain.

The Estimating Process

The team begins by looking at the story with the highest priority. The first thing to do is to have a conversation with the product owner and answer any questions about what the feature means. If the project is a game, maybe the highest-priority feature says

As a player, I want to switch between a knife and bow.

Upon further questioning of the product owner, it turns out that the bow and arrow is intended to have an ammo system, with additional arrows being found on the ground, and also that you can pull arrows out of your fallen enemies and reuse them.

The next step is a quick gut check with the team. The purpose of the gut check is to ask if it is conceivable that the feature can be completed in one sprint. If the feature is substantially bigger than one sprint, the feature needs to be broken down into two or more features that can conceivably be done in one sprint.

In the event that such a breakdown is necessary, it will require great discipline from the team and the product owner to make sure that the new stories are all actual features, not just subtasks of the big feature.

After doing a gut check, the team decides that the product owner's vision for the bow and arrow feature is just too big for the team to do in a single sprint. First, let's look at the *wrong* way to break this feature down.

Wrong

- Create the art for the bow and arrows
- Create the animations for firing the bow and for pulling the arrows out of enemies
- Program the bow mechanics.

Why is this wrong? Because if you complete only one or two of those "stories," you still don't have a feature that can be experienced in the game. Watch out for an even more devious version of this, where the tasks are phrased with AsABIWaB.

Wrong, but with AsABIWaB

- As a player, I want beautiful bow and arrow models and textures, so that I feel immersed in the game.
- As a player, I want realistic animations for firing the bow and pulling arrows out of enemies, so that I feel cool.
- As a player, I want bow and arrow mechanics to be programmed, so that the game works the way I expect.

It is true that in some sense the player wants these things. She wants to play the game after all, but she doesn't want models and animations for their own sake. She only wants them in the context of working as actual features within the game. Here's a better way to divide up the feature.

Right

- As a player, I want to have a knife as a weapon.
- As a player, I want to be able to switch to a bow (assumes unlimited ammo).
- As a player, I want to manage my arrow count and pick up arrows off the ground.
- As a player, I want to be able to rip out arrows from fallen enemies and reuse them.

Each of these stories represents a complete feature that can be experienced by the player as building blocks. Yes, only when all four of these stories are complete will the product owners' original vision have been met, but useful feedback can be gained all along the way.

After dividing up the stories this way, the team does another gut check and they think these stories represent increments of work that can be done in a sprint or less.

Before moving forward, the team asks the product owner to place the new features in order of priority. Maybe that looks like this

- As a player, I want to be able to rip out arrows from fallen enemies and reuse them.
- As a player, I want to be able to switch to a bow (assumes unlimited ammo).
- As a player, I want to have a knife as a weapon.
- As a player, I want to manage my arrow count and pick up arrows off the ground.

Now, we have an interesting challenge. The product owner has said that ripping arrows out of enemies is more important than firing them in the first place. Isn't that story dependent on the bow and arrow being implemented first?

The answer is, of course, maybe. Certainly, the traditional thing to do would be to treat the tasks as dependent and implement the bow and arrow system first, followed by the ripping out system.

But because we are doing scrum, we want to at least think about ways to deliver the highest priority value sooner. So we have a discussion with the product owner. We ask her if she thinks that it's important that what you rip out of the enemy be arrows that your character fired previously, or if you could rip out something else that you didn't necessarily put there yourself.

The product owner says that what she thinks is the most unique thing about this game is ripping things out of your enemies. The team discusses it a little bit more and decides that instead of implementing a bow or knife first, it would fit with the story for the enemies to have weak spots, represented by crystals sticking out of their bodies. Initially, the player could *only* fight the enemies by ripping these crystals out. But the product owner still thinks that eventually it would be fun to have the knife and bow and arrow systems implemented.

So now our product backlog lists the top priorities like so

- As a player, I want to rip crystals out of my enemies.
- As a player, I want to be able to switch to a bow (assumes unlimited ammo).
- As a player, I want to be able to rip out arrows from fallen enemies and reuse them.
- As a player, I want to have a knife as a weapon.
- As a player, I want to manage my arrow count and pick up arrows off the ground.

As you can see, being agile led us to change the game, and, if the product owner is right, to change the game in a way that will be exciting to players. This is something that never would have happened if we'd simply given ourselves unlimited time to build the product owners' original feature list and started breaking down tasks accordingly.

Now It's Time for a Breakdown

Now that the highest-priority features are sprint-sized, it's time to consider the tasks that go into making the feature a reality. The team spends a few minutes and comes up with the following list:

- Create the enemy model
- Create the enemy texture
- Animate the enemy walking
- Animate the enemy attacking
- Animate the enemy getting a crystal ripped out
- Animate the enemy dying
- Program the enemy AI

- Create the player model
- Create the player texture
- Animate the player walking
- Animate the player attacking
- Create a player attacking sound
- Program the user interface for controlling the player
- Test all these for quality

One note, even in this simple example, an experienced developer would quickly see that I haven't been comprehensive in my breakdown. For example, I have made no reference to sound effects and music. I've also talked about enemies dying but have not made specific reference to a health system, and I haven't contemplated the possibility of player death.

Definition of Done

While it's important to us to build something that works, we also want it to work well. Buggy code, shoddy art, and other elements can sometimes work for the purposes of a demo, but in reality the team is only deceiving itself if it considers such a sprint complete. To avoid such a scenario, scrum teams create a list of certain things that have to be done before any task can really be considered complete. This list is called the definition of done, or DoD.

Definition of Done—A checklist that must be complete before a task can be considered complete.

For instance, a DoD may specify that files have to be named a certain way or uploaded to a certain drive. Maybe you have to write unit tests or documentation. Maybe you have to convert things from one format to another.

In the case of our game example, just because the code has been written to allow a player to control their character and a proper demo can be shown to the product owner or even an end user, it doesn't mean the team considers the work done.

The DoD is a two-part checklist to help team members remember to complete any additional steps typically associated with finishing a task. First, there is a generic checklist that should describe any quality control processes or other steps that must be completed before a typical task can be considered done.

Additionally, certain tasks may have irregular extra requirements that need to be completed before they are considered done. Such specifics are also included in the DoD for a task and should be noted on the task itself.

How Many Beans Are in This Jar?

With each of these tasks broken down, the next step is to estimate them in story points, keeping in mind both the broad DoD as well as any task-specific DoDs. After that, the team might have something like the following:

- Create the enemy model—1 story point
- Create the enemy texture—1 story point
- Animate the enemy walking—2 story points
- Animate the enemy attacking—4 story points
- Animate the enemy getting a crystal ripped out—4 story points
- Animate the enemy dying—2 story points
- Program the enemy AI—4 story points
- Create the player model—1 story point
- Create the player texture—1 story point
- Animate the player walking—2 story points
- Animate the player attacking—2 story points
- Program the user interface for controlling the player—2 story points
- Test all these for quality—2 story points

All told, it looks like this first story is going to take 28 story points. If the team has substantially more than 28 points of capacity in the sprint, they'll repeat this process for as many stories as are necessary.

A team of experienced people that is accustomed to estimating with story points, but that is working together for the first time, can probably estimate 5–10 stories per hour during the sprint planning meeting. And that number might grow to 15–20 over time. For teams with inexperienced members who aren't familiar with story points, it might take over an hour just to get one story estimated.

Planning Poker

In scrum, we want the entire team to participate in the estimating process because team members with different talents may bring up aspects of a story that other team members wouldn't be aware of and that may make a story more or less complex than initially thought. However, getting many people's input into every single story and task can be a cumbersome process. We've all been in a meeting with a person, who loves to hear themselves talk.

Scrum experts have turned the estimating process into a game called "planning poker" that makes it easy to figure out where there is consensus, where there is disagreement, and to move quickly through items where everyone is on the same page while having productive discussion about items where there is disagreement.

> **Planning Poker**—A system for estimating tasks by having all team members secretly estimate a task and then reveal their estimates simultaneously.

Planning poker is played as follows:

1. Every person on the scrum team gets a deck of special cards. The cards have story point values, typically either in powers of two or the Fibonacci sequence.
2. A task is selected.
3. Each person picks a card to represent their estimate of the task.
4. Everyone shows the card at the same time. You want to avoid the first person's choice influencing the choice of the people who follow.
5. If everyone is in agreement, accept the estimate and move on.
6. If there is disagreement, the outliers share why their estimate was higher or lower than that of other team members. This will likely result in many people modifying their estimates (hopefully all converging on a central value).
7. Repeat steps 3–5 until there is general consensus. Unanimity is good, but not required. If after a few rounds three people estimate a task at a 1, and two people estimate the same task at a 2, it is acceptable to agree to 1.5, or to just go with 2 as the more conservative estimate.

Taking on Work

Once the highest-priority story has been broken down, it's time for the team members to take responsibility for tasks. In a waterfall environment, a project manager would dole out the tasks or have the lead of each department give tasks to their underlings.

It works slightly different in a scrum environment. Instead, team members take work onto their own plates, either because they are particularly interested in the task or because they think they are best suited to accomplish it efficiently. While it's a subtle difference, it results in team members being more engaged and excited about their work.

Team members take responsibility for tasks from the highest-priority story and put them in the sprint log until all of the tasks from that story have been accepted, and only then do they move on to the next story. No one can do work from the second story if the first story has not been completely loaded into the sprint log, and so on.

This last point may prove particularly difficult for teams that are imbalanced. If a team has an abundance of server programming talent and relatively little client programming talent, the team may be tempted to dip into the server-side code for the second, third, and fourth priorities, while the client-side team doesn't have enough bandwidth to finish the first priority. Avoid this temptation.

Having one element of a project get far ahead of the other elements limits flexibility. After completion of the highest-priority items, the product owner may realize that the product needs to pivot in order to reach the goal. If substantial work has been done on lower-priority features, there will be resistance to scrapping that work to pursue the new top priority. Additionally, team collaboration will be negatively affected, because the people who are working on lower-priority stories won't be able to get feedback from the other disciplines that are focused on delivering the top priority. Finally, knowing that you need talent in a particular area to get the high priorities complete may be a great opportunity for one of the team members to cross-train and expand their skills.

Modifications for ScrumButt

If you are mathematically inclined, you may remember that an ideal team size is 5 and an ideal sprint length is 2 weeks. In a full-time work environment that allows only 25% of the work day for meetings, checking e-mail, potty breaks, etc., that translates to a maximum of 300 man-hours per sprint.

As such, if you've got a part-time team of five students who can each put in 6 hours per week on your project, you can only get 60 man-hours into a

2-week sprint. Should you extend your sprint length to 10 weeks in order to have the same 300 hours that a full-time team has in a sprint?

Not to mention, because you are students, you probably can't get as much done as a team of professionals can in the same amount of time. So should you increase your sprint length to 20 weeks, so that you can get in 600 man-hours, and hopefully get as much work done as a team of professionals can get done in 2 weeks?

Regardless of your rationale, I strongly caution you against choosing sprint lengths that are excessively long. The longer a team goes without seeing the product come together in a functional state, the more opportunity there is for fear and doubt to creep in. Additionally, if you have a slacker on your team, they can lead you on for a very long time, and their laziness will only become apparent at the end of the sprint when you try and integrate their work into a coherent whole. For this reason, you might be surprised to find out that I'm personally a big fan of sprint lengths of just 1 week for teams that are heavily comprised of novices, whether students, hobbyists, or otherwise.

In asking teams not to have long sprint lengths, I recognize that I am also doing something very demanding. For many projects, it can be difficult to identify a coherent feature that could be completed in 30 man-hours or less (five people at 6 hours per week). That's like giving a professional team a sprint length of a single day. Not to mention that all of the ceremonies of scrum now take up a disproportionate amount of time relative to working time when the man-hours in a sprint are low. It is my feeling that *generally* the psychological and accountability gains of short sprint lengths outweigh the potential productivity and feature selection gains of sprint lengths with more man-hours. But you will have to decide what's right for your team, given the experience and temperament of your team members.

Next, having all team members estimate tasks is the ideal solution because it is an opportunity to have the conversations that will clarify what is involved in completing a task and making sure that everyone thinks the estimates are reasonable. For a virtual team with experienced members, I definitely recommend sticking to this scrum tradition.

However, teams with inexperienced members may find that such individuals have a very difficult time participating meaningfully and effectively in planning discussions. Similarly, they may have trouble estimating their own capacity for task completion during a sprint and therefore struggle to take work out of the product backlog onto their own plates.

In such situations, it is appropriate to have senior team members take primary responsibility for task estimation, and also to assign work to members who are in learning mode. This modification should always be done with an eye toward empowering junior team members to become proficient in estimating tasks and understanding their own capacity in future sprint planning sessions. Therefore, such members should still observe the estimation process and the task-loading process and should be encouraged to chime in whenever they have something to say.

The Bottom Line

In scrum, teams ultimately have to estimate their work and have a plan for completing it, just like any other project management approach. However, scrum focuses on breaking down tasks that are going to be completed in the very short term. Student and virtual teams are some of the biggest beneficiaries of this approach, and any modifications should be considered temporary, and made with an eye for empowering team members to become proficient in the planning process.

ScrumButt Thinking

1. Go to the section "Now It's Time for a Breakdown." Can you think of other tasks that would probably be necessary to bring this game idea to life that haven't been discussed yet? What other things might the definition of done include?
2. What are the pros and cons of having shorter sprint times?
3. Who on your team is prepared for sprint planning, and who needs some time to learn the ropes?

ScrumButt NOW!

1. Open the ScrumButt resources workbook.
2. Find the planning poker worksheet, and print 1 set of cards for each superhero on your team.
3. Find the product backlog worksheet.
4. Play planning poker to estimate the first few stories, enough to cover the capacity of one to two sprints.

5. If your first story is larger than 1 sprint, divide it into multiple stories.

6. Copy 1 sprint's worth of stories to the sprint log worksheet.

7. Break down each story into tasks.

8. Play planning poker again to estimate the individual tasks. Place the agreed upon number in the initial estimate column.

9. Set the work remaining column equal to the initial estimate column.

10. Have every superhero select enough tasks to fill their personal capacity.

11. Call someone a ScrumButt and explain that it's a compliment.

9

The Fifth Secret of Scrum
The ScrumMaster and Scrum Coach

> The first responsibility of a leader is to define reality. The last is to say thank you. In between, the leader is a servant.
>
> **Max de Pree**

Chapter in a Tweet

The ScrumMaster makes sure the team is following scrum and helps people who get stuck.

The Supreme Court Justice

Project management methodologies are essentially about governing a project in such a way that it's successful, much like a national government is about managing a society so that it has successful outcomes. To understand the role of the ScrumMaster, it can be helpful to revisit the things you probably learned in grade school about how the government works.

Most successful modern governments are established on the idea that it works well for power and responsibility to be distributed between many people. This system is often called checks and balances. In the United States, national power is divided between the executive, legislative, and judicial branches. This division is set forth in the Constitution. In Scrum, the agile manifesto is like the preamble to the Constitution. The best practices described in this book are the articles. And the ScrumButt modifications are the constitutional amendments. I am George Washington, and you are Paul Revere. Ok, that last part might be going overboard.

The product owner, though only one person, is best compared to Congress. By defining the priorities, they set the agenda that the executive branch is expected to follow. The scrum team is best compared to the executive branch. They bring to life the vision of the legislative branch by doing whatever is necessary, in accordance with the Constitution.

The ScrumMaster, you've no doubt deduced, is compared to the judicial branch. The judicial branch doesn't make laws, and they don't enforce laws. Rather, they make sure that the actions of both branches are legal and settle any disputes. Similarly, the ScrumMaster makes sure that the product owner and scrum team play the game according to the rules. If either group starts to stray away from the principles of scrum, the ScrumMaster reins them in. It's like issuing a ruling.

A Judge Needs Good Judgment

Given the comparison to a supreme court justice, it's not surprising that one of the most important characteristics of the ScrumMaster is good judgment. Ultimately, the quality of the ScrumMaster is going to play a critical role in determining the degree to which a team successfully implements scrum.

The first area where the ScrumMaster will exercise judgment is in determining if a violation has occurred. Violations generally take the following forms:

1. The product owner tries to create stories in a way to dictate how the scrum team should work, rather than expressing the feature priorities.
2. The team tries to work on tasks that do not contribute to the highest-priority stories.
3. The team wants to dispense with or significantly alter one of the ceremonies or best practices of scrum.

Sometimes, it will be easy to recognize these infractions, but other times the infraction can be subtle and will sneak past someone who isn't very observant. This is especially true in the case of ScrumMasters who are new to scrum themselves.

The second area in which a ScrumMaster must exercise judgment is in picking her battles. A team that is new to scrum is invariably going to commit multiple violations of scrum principles during their first few sprints as they try to get a handle both on the project and on their new project management approach. As described previously, it is the job of the ScrumMaster to note and correct these issues. However, if she tries to correct every violation she sees, she risks demotivating the team and slowing progress down, rather than tapping into the power of scrum to improve the pace of a project, its outcomes, and the satisfaction of the people who work on it.

This can be a tight balancing act. Some teams find implementing scrum to be very easy and natural. A ScrumMaster on these teams may only notice a few scrum violations during any given sprint, and the team may respond positively to when the ScrumMaster takes steps to help the team correct their actions. On other teams, violations will be plentiful, and some team members will be very resistant to suggestions for improvement.

A wise ScrumMaster thinks about how urgently an issue needs to be solved in order to keep a project on track. If it needs to be solved immediately, she brings it up immediately. If it can wait without derailing the project, she waits. We haven't talked about them yet, but the sprint retrospective is a built-in opportunity for the ScrumMaster (and other team members) to address any issues that occurred during the prior sprint.

More Servant than Master

The *master* part of ScrumMaster doesn't refer to the ScrumMaster's relationship with other team members. Instead, it refers to the ScrumMaster's relationship with the principles of scrum. More than anyone else in the team, the ScrumMaster needs to know how scrum is supposed to work, and how to persuade her team to tap into its benefits. This persuasive aspect of the ScrumMaster's roles cannot be overstated. According to scrum, the ScrumMaster doesn't have a mechanism to compel someone to stop or start doing something. Rather, the ScrumMaster provides data about a team's effectiveness and inspires them to improve. In this role of an inspiring data provider, the ScrumMaster is clearly serving her team.

There is one other major aspect of service to the ScrumMaster role, that of a general problem solver. Throughout a project, things will happen that threaten the scrum team's productivity. Maybe there is an Internet outage.

Maybe a certain vendor will become unresponsive. Maybe a piece of equipment breaks down.

These kinds of challenges could theoretically be solved by anyone in the team, but by having the ScrumMaster focus on all these unanticipated issues, it frees up the rest of the team to focus on doing their work. Certainly, the ScrumMaster may seek input from other team members in order to solve some of these problems, but by having primary responsibility for these issues rest with the ScrumMaster you achieve the highest likelihood that the rest of the team will achieve peak productivity.

Interruption Interceptor

Speaking of productivity, the ScrumMaster has one other responsibility that will make sure the rest of the team performs at their maximum potential. Nothing kills productivity quite like unexpected interruptions, and the ScrumMaster is tasked with doing what he can to minimize such interruptions with his team.

Depending on the environment, this could take several forms. In professional environments without a front desk/admin, the ScrumMaster might do things like answer the phone and sign for packages. More importantly, the ScrumMaster frequently serves as the single contact point for external teams and management. Particularly, talented teammates may be enlisted so often to help with other projects that they struggle to find enough time to fulfill their responsibility to their primary team. By requiring other teams to contact the ScrumMaster, instead of directly contacting the team member, the ScrumMaster is frequently able to time and prioritize such inquiries in a way that the external team's needs are met without jeopardizing primary responsibilities.

Another group of people that are infamous for derailing the scrum train are managers external to the scrum team. They are known for calling emergency meetings, unexpectedly changing priorities, and otherwise doing things that distract scrum teams from bringing a product owner's vision to life. As with external teams, by training managers to work with ScrumMasters, such interruptions and changes can frequently be avoided entirely. The ScrumMaster can often attend emergency meetings for the team and loop them in later when it is more convenient. Similarly, he may be able to work with management to implement changes in a way that reduces or eliminates the opportunity for such changes to distract the scrum team.

Good Teams Have Good Coaches

While every role in scrum benefits from experience, emotional intelligence, and strategic thinking, the role of a ScrumMaster is particularly demanding of these features. When introducing new teams to scrum, a ScrumMaster with all these traits may be able to carry the rest of the team while everyone else gets up to speed.

However, most teams that are new to scrum are also going to have a ScrumMaster who is new to scrum. You can imagine that such a ScrumMaster could struggle to help her team implement scrum, even if the team is very eager to do things right.

Enter the scrum coach. A scrum coach is a scrum expert, usually someone who has been practicing scrum for many years, frequently having previously held all the three roles: product owner, team member, and ScrumMaster. The scrum coach doesn't take an official role in the team but rather observes the team. When he spots a problem, he works through the members of the team to help get the project on track.

Most frequently, the scrum coach will work through the ScrumMaster. After all, the ScrumMaster is supposed to notice such issues and move the team toward resolution on her own. By working through her, the scrum coach teaches her to spot problems, evaluate which problems are most pressing, and understand how to best achieve change. However, sometimes the scrum coach will work directly with a product owner to help them formulate better stories or think critically about prioritization choices. At other times, the scrum coach will work directly with a team member to help evolve their estimating skills or work habits.

Modifications for ScrumButt

The ScrumMaster makes sure you are practicing scrum, as opposed to claiming to practice scrum while actually practicing something else. In the case of ScrumButt, the ScrumMaster's role becomes more important, not less so. Because you know that you are going to be ignoring at least a few key tenets of scrum, it becomes that much more important to make sure that you are very intentional about sticking to scrum in most other aspects and have incredibly well thought out reasons for making any further modifications to scrum best practices. As such, don't tinker with the role of the ScrumMaster.

Similarly, it is highly advisable for student and virtual teams to seek a scrum coach. The scrum coach isn't officially a ScrumButt modification, since it is something that is optionally practiced even by very experienced, colocated teams who want to make sure their transition to scrum goes off without a hitch. However, the value of a coach is even more apparent when teams are trying to implement a custom flavor of scrum that substantially departs from the norm.

The Bottom Line

One of the reasons scrum works is because there is an entire role dedicated to making sure that the benefits of scrum are being realized. ScrumMaster is a challenging role, but also one that is very rewarding!

ScrumButt Thinking

1. How does your team feel about implementing scrum? What implications does this have for the ScrumMaster?
2. What qualities do you have that would make you a good ScrumMaster? In what ways could you stand to improve?

ScrumButt NOW!

1. Open the ScrumButt resources workbook.
2. Find the ScrumButt team members' worksheet.
3. Fill in the name of your ScrumMaster.
4. If applicable, fill in the name of your scrum coach.
5. Give someone a high five in the next 5 minutes. If you have to put on clothes and go outside, you'd better get to it!

10

The Sixth Secret of Scrum
Daily Stand-Ups

Truth is confirmed by inspection.

Tacitus

Chapter in a Tweet

By sharing what you've done, what you're doing, and what's in your way, everyone can help you hit your goals.

One Day at a Time

One of the things we've criticized consistently throughout this book is how waterfall project management tries to make long-term predictions based on early assumptions that aren't typically accurate over long periods of time. We've also criticized waterfall for creating an environment of day-to-day micromanagement as project leaders try to hold the development team accountable for the long-term plan.

In scrum, we've identified that our "long-term" thinking is primarily centered on the sprint. But scrum also addresses the need for short-term planning and coordination to reach our sprint goals with daily stand-up meetings.

Why Stand-Up?

In general, meetings are universally reviled as being boring, unnecessary timewasters. The last thing we want to do in scrum is institutionalize a ceremony that is perceived as a time suck by the people who are expected to attend it.

One key to having an effective meeting is to keep it short. And one way to keep everyone in the room focused on wrapping the meeting up quickly is to have everyone stand up for the entire duration of the meeting.

Yes, by convention, everyone who attends a stand-up meeting literally stays on their feet the whole time. It's not that big of a deal though, because there's no reason for a stand-up to go more than 15 minutes. A good stand-up can even get knocked out in 5–10 minutes. Teams that want to create even more incentive to end stand-up meetings quickly can require all members to hold a handstand against the wall for the duration of the meeting. *Author's note—I haven't tested this, but it makes sense, right?

> Another name for the daily stand-up is the daily scrum. This is a great excuse to say the word scrum on a daily basis at a minimum, which is guaranteed to raise morale.

Now that we've talked about what it's called and why, let's talk about what actually happens in the meeting.

The Attendees

The daily scrum is a meeting that belongs to the developers, and they are the ones who will drive it. That said, the product owner and ScrumMaster also need to attend, for reasons that will be outlined in the following text.

Some people who aren't on the scrum team may be interested in keeping tabs on the project, such as investors, owners, and clients. Anyone who wants to is invited to attend the daily stand-up, but only the scrum team is allowed to participate. Inviting others to share their thoughts or otherwise interact during the stand-up will definitely jeopardize the team's ability to keep the meeting to 15 minutes or less.

COMMITTED OR INVOLVED

A pig and a chicken live on a farm together and become good friends. One day, they get to talking about entrepreneurship, and the pig brings up the idea of opening a restaurant.

"That's a great idea!" said the chicken.

"I'm glad you think so," said the pig. "But I've been wracking my brain trying to think of a good name."

"How about ham and eggs?"

"No thanks," said the pig. "I'd be committed but you'd only be involved."

When it comes to the stand-up meeting, the team members are committed, but managers, owners, investors, and others are designated as just involved. At the daily stand-up, only committed team members are allowed to speak.

Fortunately, no one on your scrum team is being asked to give up their life for someone's breakfast.

The 3 Whatchus

The agenda for the stand-up meeting is built around having each superhero take a turn answering three basic questions.

Whatchu Done?

For the first question, the developer will explain what she's accomplished since the last stand-up. If it's the first stand-up of the sprint, you can skip this question. The superhero doesn't need to go into detail, just share a quick overview of the progress she's made on the tasks she's working on. The developer should also update the sprint log with an accurate estimate in the work remaining section on the tasks she's worked on.

Importantly, if a superhero begins a task and realizes that it's more complicated than was initially projected, she may need to update the work remaining to a number that is higher than the initial estimate, despite the fact that she's already put time into it. Having an accurate number in the work remaining section of the sprint log is essential to successfully completing a sprint.

WhatchuDoin'?

For the second question, the developer briefly explains what activities she is going to complete prior to the next stand-up meeting. Scrum practitioners believe in the power of focus, and it's traditional to complete one task before moving onto another, rather than working simultaneously on multiple tasks.

Additionally, in order to hold each other accountable, scrum teams make sure that their superheroes are specific about the work that will be completed before the next stand-up, not simply to say what she'll be working on. The difference is subtle but it's important. Here's an example of the difference.

LessEffective: "I'll be working on the UI for the sign-up page. I should have it done 3 days from now."

More Effective: "Before the next stand-up, I'll have written the instructional text that the user will see immediately before the sign-up form. I'll also have written fun default text for the sign-up fields. And I'll create three versions of the submit button for the product owner to choose from."

The reason that the first one isn't ideal is because a team member who is struggling can hide behind the ambiguity of the first statement and claim to be productive when in fact he hasn't made the progress he expected. At the next stand-up, even if he has essentially done nothing, he might report, "I worked on the sign-up UI like I said, and I'm going to be working on it more today."

Contrast this with the second example. If he gets held up by some task, it'll be very hard to hide. He would have to say, "I tried to brainstorm some really creative intro copy and default field text, but I spent too much time on it and didn't come up with anything I like. However, I did design the three versions of the submit button I promised." With this specific information, the team will have a better feel for how much closer they are to their goals, and how productive each team member is.

If a superhero consistently falls short of his predictions, the ScrumMaster may need to have a conversation with him to find out how his productivity can be improved. Alternatively, maybe he is very productive, but not very skilled at estimating what he can get done between stand-ups. Either way, by having insight into everyone's productivity, the team prevents small problems from becoming big delays.

Whatchu 'Fraid Of?

During a sprint, things will come up. Computers will crash, deliveries will come late, people will get sick, and so on. During every stand-up, superheroes take the opportunity to share anything that is preventing them from moving forward as expected.

This is the reason that the product owner and ScrumMaster attend the meeting. The ScrumMaster takes ownership of anything that is brought up during this part of the meeting and makes sure to find a timely resolution. This frees up the superhero to continue working on the project, instead of putting out fires. In the case of certain technical issues, the ScrumMaster may not be able to solve the problem herself, but she ensures that any meetings, mentorship opportunities, or external vendor requests are properly set up to keep the project moving forward.

Sometimes, what will be preventing a developer from moving forward is the fact that she doesn't understand exactly what the product owner wants regarding a particular feature. For example, there may be an element of the UI for which a color must be chosen, but which was not discussed during sprint planning. By being in attendance, the product owner can offer quick clarifications or set up meetings with the superheroes as appropriate.

The most important thing to remember, and the hardest thing to truly do, is to remember that the stand-up meeting is *not* the time to actually solve the superheroes' fears. The stand-up meeting is only used to make everyone on the team aware of the challenges their teammates face. Once the team is aware, solutions should be discussed and pursued outside the meeting. This may mean immediately *after* the stand-up, but it definitely doesn't mean *during* the stand-up.

The Burndown

Burndown is what scrum teams do to superheroes who don't do what they say during the WatchuDoin' part of the stand-up meeting.

Psych!

The burndown chart is actually a simple, visual representation of the team's progress toward completing the sprint backlog. The chart tracks the work remaining in the sprint over time. Naturally, the object is to get the work remaining to 0 before the end of the sprint.

The vertical axis represents the work remaining in the sprint, ideally measured in story points. The horizontal axis represents time, in stand-up meetings. Typically, a burndown chart has two lines: one of them represents a forecast that represents smooth and even progress from day 1 of the sprint to the last day, and the other line is the actual work remaining, which is likely to be substantially more erratic, as teams will find that some days are more productive than others.

If you're using software, the burndown chart may be updated in real time. Otherwise, the burndown is typically updated by the ScrumMaster immediately after every stand-up. Unlike many business graphs in which people want to see the line going up over time, such as a sales chart, with a burndown chart you want to see the line going down... burning down, if you will. Here are some examples of burndown charts (Figures 10.1 through 10.4).

FIGURE 10.1
The Initial State of a Burndown.

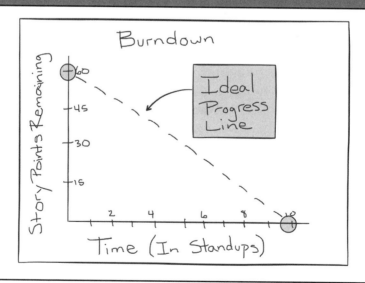

FIGURE 10.2
A Burndown Where Some of the Tasks Were Improperly Estimated during Sprint Planning, Resulting in More Work Remaining on Day 2 than on Day 1.

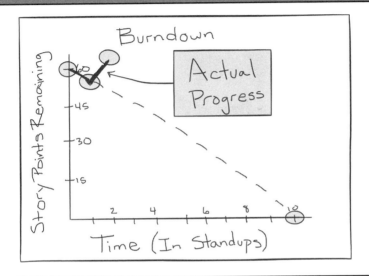

FIGURE 10.3
A Typical Burndown about Halfway through a Sprint.

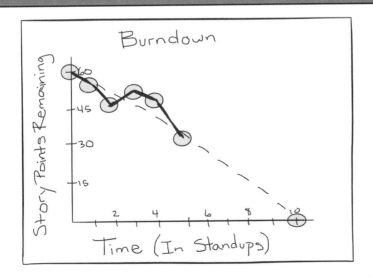

FIGURE 10.4
A Burndown for a Team that Successfully Completed Their Sprint Backlog.

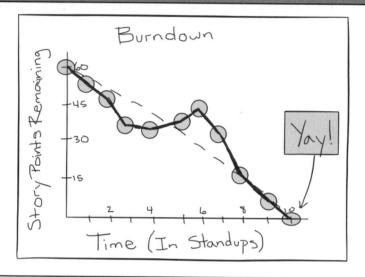

Ahead or Behind

Using the burndown chart, it's easy to tell if your team is ahead of schedule or behind schedule during a sprint. If the latest point on the actual line is above the points on the ideal line, then you are behind schedule. If the actual point is below the ideal point, you are ahead of schedule.

The Nuclear Option

The point of organizing work into sprints is for project teams to make relatively small commitments about their project timeline over a short period of time without having to make grand predictions about what the project will look like months or years down the road. In exchange, developers are expected to deliver on their sprint goals.

However, teams that are new to scrum, new to the project, new to working together, new to the industry, etc., may fall behind schedule, especially during their first few sprints. In fact, they may fall so far behind schedule that it becomes rather obvious that there is no chance that the team will get back on schedule by the end of the sprint. This can even happen to experienced scrum teams.

When this happens, *there is no good option*. If this happens to you and you're the sort of person to beat yourself up, you'd be perfectly justified in really laying into yourself for letting this happen to your team. It'd be perfectly reasonable for you to reenact that scene in Fight Club where Edward Norton literally beats himself up in boss's office, drawing blood and breaking things.

OK. Maybe you shouldn't hurt yourself, but this is a really big deal, and you need to make sure your team doesn't make a habit of it. If you miss your sprint goal, you had one or more of the following problems:

- You didn't know how to plan your work.
- You didn't know how to calculate your capacity.
- You didn't know how to estimate tasks and stories.
- You didn't have the technical ability to do (or learn to do) what you said you would.

If you have these problems regularly, you will be perceived as untrustworthy. If you're working for someone else, you might lose the project. If you're working on a passion project, the team may lose confidence in itself and abandon the project before it is complete. Clearly, these are serious consequences you want to avoid.

But since it did happen, you need to deal with it. There are really only two options.

Option 1—You keep the workload the same and lengthen the sprint.
Option 2—You put some work from the sprint backlog back into the product backlog and hold your sprint time consistent.

I strongly discourage you from pursuing option 1. When you start to change the length of the sprint, you start playing with fire. First off, you may be messing up people's schedules. For example, if you usually end sprints on Fridays and do sprint planning the following Monday, by adding on 1 day, you now have to move sprint planning. Depending on the nature of your team, this might be very difficult.

Another reason I don't like changing the sprint length is because it can lead to teams thinking that missing sprint goals isn't that bad. If you only add on 1 day to the end of your two-week sprint, it's not that big a deal, is it?

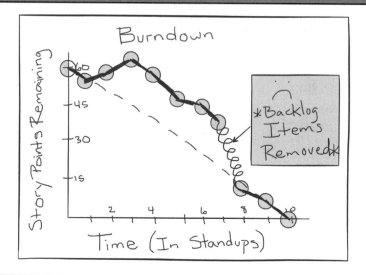

FIGURE 10.5
A Burndown for a Team That Had to Alter Their Sprint Backlog.

It is. Whether you add on 1 day or 1 month, you missed your sprint goal, and you can't do that consistently.

Option 2 is the lesser of the evils because it honors the importance of consistent sprint lengths, but it also teaches teams an important lesson that can be used in future sprint plans. By removing 1 or more stories from the sprint, the team learns how much work they really can fit in a sprint. This is knowledge that they can use in future sprint planning sessions.

When you take an item out of the sprint backlog, the work remaining will automatically drop. It's important that the burndown be annotated such that the team doesn't get credit for having a really productive day. Here's an example of what that might look like (Figure 10.5).

The Angel Option

Just as teams can get incredibly behind schedule, they can also get incredibly ahead of schedule. If that happens, you have a few options. Honestly, I recommend that you use the extra time to reward the team. Paid days off, a team-building outing, and similar activities all seem appropriate to me.

FIGURE 10.6
A Burndown for a Team That Got ahead of Schedule and Added Work to the Sprint Backlog.

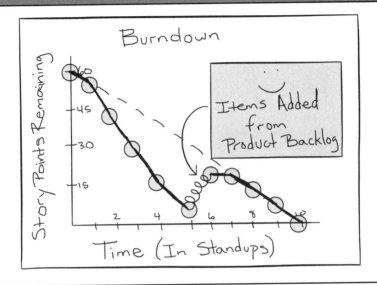

However, if such incentives aren't possible in your environment, or if you have a team of workaholics, you can essentially do the opposite of the nuclear option. Again, I strongly discourage you from shortening the sprint length and beginning the next sprint ahead of schedule. Instead, you can take 1 or more stories off the product backlog and put them into the sprint backlog. Make sure the burndown is annotated to give the team credit for the awesome job they've done (Figure 10.6).

Modifications for ScrumButt

Stand-up meetings are a core scrum practice. Keeping them short will keep you effective. I've never encountered a situation where I thought a team should solve problems during the meeting, use the meeting for planning, or eliminate stand-ups altogether.

There are two situations that might require modification for student and virtual teams. The first is the case where team members do not have overlapping schedules. First, I do encourage you to look closely and see if there are any opportunities for aligning schedules. If that's not possible, you might conduct virtual, asynchronous stand-ups. Basically, each team member sends an e-mail to the other team members answering the threeWhatchus. Typically, asynchronous teams will have a deadline by when each stand-up needs to be shared.

One other aspect of the stand-up that can be slightly modified is the interval. Some teams may get together to work every other night for 4 hours. If that's the case, you can get by with having a stand-up every other day. Other teams may work for 20 hours over a Saturday and Sunday and feel like they should have multiple stand-ups each working day. If you make a modification of this sort, there should be no more than 8 working hours between stand-ups.

THE DAY SPRINT

In one of the courses I taught we were working on a game project and had decided in sprint intervals of 1 week. This course had the peculiar feature of a 6-hour work session once per week (in exchange for no official homework or exams). Outside of this work session, students weren't expected to work directly on the project but were rather expected to do any research they needed to do to be properly prepared for the work session.

Rather than having a single stand-up for the whole day, and rather than having a stand-up every single day when there was really only one productive day each week, we had 3 stand-up meetings during the work sessions; at the start, 2 hours in, and 4 hours in.

Because many students have difficulty estimating tasks even on that short a scale, the stand-up was predictably a very valuable opportunity to see where roadblocks were starting to form, to get senior students to help struggling students where possible, and to reallocate forces as necessary.

Without the stand-up, I'm very confident students wouldn't admit to having trouble until the 5th hour of the sprint. Because of the stand-up, we were able to see trouble brewing after only a couple hours, and many students would seek help even before the official stand-up if they had the sense that their work was going slower than anticipated and was going to affect the rest of the team. This helped us reach maximum effectiveness and prevented struggling students from flying under the radar, which is a frequent challenge in group projects across academic settings.

The Bottom Line

By now you may have noticed something. When it comes to getting things done, scrum is a cold-hearted bastard! It doesn't care how hard you've worked and for how long. Rather, scrum only cares how much work you have left to complete what you said you would.

The stand-up meeting is how scrum teams coordinate work to make sure they reach their goals, avoid surprises, and deal with them quickly when they can't be avoided.

ScrumButt Thinking

1. In addition to the burndown, what other charts or information might be useful for the scrum team to review regularly.
2. Do you think the 3 Whatchus are the ideal questions for a stand-up? Should there be more or fewer questions?

ScrumButt NOW!

1. Open the ScrumButt resources workbook.
2. Find the Burndown Chart worksheet.
3. Fill in the actual and target work remaining with the story points of your sprint.
4. Fill in the target work remaining cells with values to create a straight line that ends at 0 at the end of your sprint.
5. Update the actual work remaining with the figure from the "total work remaining" cell in the sprint backlog worksheet after every stand-up.
6. Find a rooftop. Scream out, "I love scrum, and I don't care who knows it!"

11

The Seventh Secret of Scrum
Sprint Reviews and Retrospectives

Perfection is not attainable, but if we chase perfection we can catch excellence.

Vince Lombardi

Chapter in a Tweet

The Sprint Review is a meeting to improve the product. The Sprint Retrospective is a meeting to improve how we work on the product.

Having worked hard on a daily basis to bring the next phase of the project to life, it's time to review progress. In scrum, there are actually two types of progress in which we are interested. First, we're obviously excited to see how the project itself turned out. Second, we want to analyze our working habits to make sure that we are adhering to scrum processes and that our work habits that aren't prescribed by scrum are making us as effective as possible.

The Sprint Review

The sprint review is open to anyone who wants to attend and is probably the most exciting and worthwhile meeting for people to attend who aren't involved in the project on a daily basis. This is because the sprint review is kind of like show and tell. Investors, owners, managers, customers, and everyone else are infinitely more excited to see a product in action, than they are to hear about forecasts, challenges, etc.

Demonstration

In general, the first step of the sprint review is to demonstrate the product. This is the joy and the beauty of scrum. In most project management systems, after a couple of weeks have gone by you probably have some code written, some art created, and some tests designed, but nothing would have been integrated, as integration is seen as a final and separate step.

In scrum, the most important trait of the sprint is that the team took the time to integrate everyone's work, and so you have a working increment of the product that you can invite people to use. You aren't showing user interface mock-ups, you are showing the user interface in the product. You aren't talking about how a piece of code will work, you are showing how it does work. You aren't making predictions about how the product will solve the user's problems, you are displaying how it already does solve some of the user's problems.

What's more difficult to display, but what is also important to discuss during the demo, is for the superhero team to confirm that each feature of the product has gone through a quality assurance process.

Acceptance

If everything has gone according to plan, the product owner was present during sprint planning to help clarify expectations. She was also present during stand-up meetings in case there were any questions that weren't fully considered during sprint planning. And she was probably available generally to answer questions about the vision of the product as they arose during the course of any given day. For this reason, the product owner probably has a pretty good idea of what she's going to see in the demo.

But occasionally, it doesn't happen that way. Maybe the product owner had other commitments that limited their attendance and availability for the standard scrum ceremonies. Alternatively, maybe despite the product owner's availability, one or more of the team members implemented their own vision for a feature, and it was at odds with the product owner's vision.

Whatever the case, at the conclusion of the demo, the product owner has to accept or reject the sprint. To accept the sprint, the product owner is verifying that the team did what they said they would do. To reject the sprint is to say that, from the product owner's perspective, the team did not do what they said they would. Fortunately, it's rare for there to be surprises during this step.

One thing that the team should keep an eye out for is that no one, particularly the product owner, attempts to suggest that more work was agreed to during sprint planning than actually was. This typically involves small elements of polish that someone thought were implicit in a request. Let me share a nontechnical example. When I was a kid, my mom asked me to put my clothes in the washing machine. So I put my clothes in the washing machine. Several hours later, my mom complained that I hadn't started the washing machine. She felt that starting the washing machine was implicit in the request to put my clothes in the washing machine. While it was probably reasonable for my mom to assume that by asking me to put my clothes in the washer I would also know to start the washer, scrum doesn't work that way. Instead, scrum only holds the superheroes responsible for work they explicitly agreed to in the definition of done.

A technical example might be something like an e-mail field in a sign-up form. Perhaps, the product owner assumed that the field would be validated to make sure that the value the user put in the field was actually an e-mail. This prevents users from purposely entering gibberish, or from accidentally typing an invalid e-mail. However, if this expectation was not discussed, and the superhero responsible for implementing the feature did not implement a validation check, the product owner could not reject the sprint for that reason, rather the product owner would accept the sprint, but would create a new backlog item for e-mail validation. The product owner would make a note to discuss this kind of expectation in the future. Additionally, this issue could potentially be discussed during the sprint retrospective, which is where the team thinks of ways to improve their working habits and modify the definition of done.

Influence

Now that the product owner has had a chance to see the project in action, she has an opportunity to modify the product backlog before the next sprint planning meeting. Capitalizing on this opportunity is perhaps the critical junction that separates good scrum teams from great scrum teams. A good team understands that having a working increment of the project at the end of every sprint is desirable simply because it keeps everyone honest and provides an opportunity to make sure there are no unexpected technical hurdles at the point of integration. A great scrum team understands that the real value of having a working version of the product at the end of every sprint is in taking the experience gained by actually using the product to develop insights into how the product can be made better. These insights, and adjustments in priority, happen in ways that couldn't have been predicted when the idea was conceived, or even when it was discussed during the last sprint planning session.

While the product owner is responsible for making changes to the product backlog, the sprint review is a powerful opportunity for other stakeholders to influence the product owner and persuade them why a new feature should be added to the backlog, or why a feature that is currently a low priority deserves to be raised to the top of the list. Because the sprint review meeting is frequently attended by people who aren't familiar with scrum, some of whom may hold positions of power over the scrum team, the product owner needs to be careful to evaluate all feedback and make sure that the final suggestions that make it onto the product backlog are consistent with scrum values.

For example, if a team is making a game, an investor may make a request to see concept art for all the levels of the game. However, this request is inconsistent with scrum, as it has one or more members of the team working on assets that will not be integrated into the game in the next sprint. Furthermore, as more progress on the game is made, the art style or ideas for levels may change. A team that has invested a heavy amount in early concept art will either be forced to abandon the work they've put a lot of time into, or to stick with using concept art that no longer represents where the team wants to go.

The scrum master and scrum coach can be valuable resources to help the product owner determine how to take feedback from stakeholders who don't speak "scrum" and convert it into useful product backlog items that are consistent with scrum values.

The Sprint Retrospective

It's been said that, "If you're not growing you're dying." Scrum practitioners believe that this highly quotable version of the second law of thermodynamics applies not only to organisms, but also to groups. To be clear, we're not talking about growth in terms of team headcount. We're talking about growth in terms of team capacity. The final ceremony of scrum, the sprint retrospective, was established to ensure that teams are continuously growing in their ability to deliver fantastic products. The sprint retrospective is run by ScrumMaster and takes the following format.

Review Velocity

You remember back in our discussion of sprint planning how we talked about using story points instead of hours to estimate tasks? Finally, we get to see the fruits of our efforts. If your team has five developers working 40-hour weeks during 2-week sprints, then you have a theoretical maximum of 200 man-hours that could have gone into the sprint, and more likely something like 160 hours. Whatever the number, from sprint to sprint that value isn't going to change. You'll plan to do 160 hours of work, and you'll either do or not do the work to which you committed.

If you aren't using story points, any feeling of progress will be qualitative at best. After five sprints, you will probably have the feeling that you are getting more done with your available hours, but you won't be able to say with any degree of confidence whether by "more" you mean 5% more, 10% more, or 50% more.

Alternatively, if you are using story points, you will be able to describe your improvements more objectively. If during your first sprint you were able to complete 10 story points with your allotted hours, and during the second sprint you were able to complete 11, then you saw 10% improvement. 10% improvement in a 2-week period is pretty awesome, but not at all uncommon with newly formed scrum teams.

By reviewing velocity first, you shape the rest of the retrospective discussion. Are you celebrating increased efficiency and trying to find ways to maintain and improve it, or did recent changes cause a drop in productivity, and you need to figure out how to reverse it?

Review Prior Retrospective Commitments

If this is your first sprint retrospective with a new team or project, skip to the next step. Otherwise, after the velocity review you'll want to follow up on your commitments from the prior sprint retrospective. It's OK for the ScrumMaster to share her own observations as well as any available objective data in relationship to the commitments. However, she should not dominate this portion of the meeting, or any other element of the meeting. Rather, she wants to find out how the team feels and shape the conversation with data and her own observations as necessary.

Ultimately, what you want to determine during this step is whether or not the team worked how they said they would work, which allows you to think critically about whether or not a change you implemented had a positive effect. For example, maybe the team decided that artists and programmers working on a particular aspect of the project should have an additional meeting every other day in order to coordinate and test their work.

Suppose further that during the next sprint velocity declines. The team may be inclined to blame the new meeting for hurting productivity. However, in reality, maybe this meeting only happened once instead of the five times that it was supposed to happen. Would the team have seen better results if they'd actually held all five meetings, or would productivity have been hit even worse? Of course, the actual answer is situation-dependent, but by recognizing how faithful the team was to their commitments from the prior retrospective, they can reduce their chances of falsely blaming or giving credit to a particular action for the changes in efficiency observed during the most recent sprint.

Start/Continue/Stop

With the team having a clear understanding of how they performed during the sprint, it's time to brainstorm ideas on how the team can improve. One proven way to elicit this kind of feedback is the Start/Continue/Stop method, or SCS. In this method, each person on the team is going to share one thing that she thinks the team should start doing, one thing she thinks the team should continue doing, and one thing she thinks the team should stop doing. Ideally, before the retrospective each member has put some thought into her SCS, rather than coming to the meeting unprepared or brainstorming on the fly.

It's important that the SCS be about team improvement, and not focused on a particular individual. Here's an example of a good SCS:

> I think every day we should assign someone to share an inspirational quote right after the stand-up, because I think everyone is energized to work hard for a few hours after hearing something inspirational. I think we should continue bringing in a masseuse for 15-minute massages on Fridays, because I think it makes everyone feel valued and want to give more to the project. I think we should stop allowing monkeys to roam

free in the office, because everyone is spending the first 30 minutes of their day cleaning poop off their desks.

In this example, every suggestion is something that impacts the team as a whole. Compare that with this example SCS:

> I think Johnny should start showing up to the office on time, because we lose 2 hours of productive time as a team just with him being late. I think Ronald should continue to bring in donuts every morning, because I love donuts and they make me work harder. I think Sue should stop eating at her desk if she's going to chew like a horse, because none of us can concentrate with that kind of noise and it takes us a long time to get back in the flow after every one of her meals and snacks.

This person isn't focused on team productivity, but rather on a combination of his own personal preferences, and also on calling out teammates for their individual habits. While the observations may be correct, the sprint retrospective isn't the place to make them. Rather, he can approach team members individually or work with the ScrumMaster to have 1-on-1 conversations with these people about their work habits.

After everyone has shared their SCS, two things will need to happen. First, the team will need to discuss any conflicts. For example, one person might have said they want to continue the practice of massages on Friday because it improves morale, while another person may have suggested stopping the practice because it takes up time and money and is distracting. The ScrumMaster needs to guide the discussion such that each side has an opportunity to make their points, but it's quite possible that neither side can be won over or persuaded, so don't feel compelled to wait for consensus.

The second thing that will need to happen is for the team to determine which of the suggestions will have the biggest benefits to productivity. There is frequently consensus around these topics, but in cases where there isn't consensus, the ScrumMaster is ultimately in charge of prioritizing the list.

Commit to Improvements

After this process, the team has probably made a list of one to three dozen items. While it would be awesome to live in a world where executing on all these items was a possibility, most teams don't have the bandwidth to make that many changes at once while remaining productive. Additionally, some of the suggestions may require money or other resources to implement what the team won't be able to get. In a way, the SCS list has become a sort of product backlog, where the team is the product. As with sprint planning, the team should start with the items that are thought to make the biggest impact and see if they can agree to implement those first. At some point, probably after agreeing to two or three changes, the team will decide that it's reached its capacity for change.

It's important to note that while the ScrumMaster runs the meeting and keeps the discussion productive, she should not mandate any changes. Rather, any changes the team undertakes should be chosen and agreed to by the team members. If there is substantial resistance to a particular change, the team should choose action items that are more universally accepted as beneficial.

Keep It Up, and Keep It Fresh

The sprint retrospective is the meeting that is most often disrespected in scrum. In particular, when a team has been working together for a while and seen a lot of improvement, they may start to lack ideas on how to improve further. They then decide that the sprint retrospective is a waste of time, and they decide to eliminate it, supposedly in favor of having more time to be productive.

That kind of decision is like a person who has been eating healthy for several months, deciding that, because he has obtained his target weight, he no longer needs to eat healthy. It is misguided and predictably results in performance dropping. In fact, sometimes performance drops so much that people attribute their initial gains to a "honeymoon" period that occurred during the beginning of scrum, but that couldn't be sustained over the long term. Teams that drop the retrospective may end up looking to abandon scrum altogether in search of some other magical product management pill to make things better. Of course, you and I know that if they had just kept doing scrum, of which retrospectives are an integral part, they would have continued to improve and eliminated bad habits that crept in after retrospectives were dropped. Scrum didn't fail them, they failed scrum.

While the sprint retrospective itself is an inviolable component of scrum, the way that the team runs the discussion is flexible. While the SCS method is a good way to run the meeting that may work for some teams indefinitely, it may become stale. It is the ScrumMaster's duty to make sure that retrospectives feel productive, and she is free to explore other avenues for facilitating frank and meaningful discussion about the team's practices. Entire books have been written on the topic of running great sprint retrospectives, and the Internet also has many resources.

Modifications for ScrumButt

The sprint review is the cake of scrum. The team made something that works! Looking at it, celebrating it, and deciding how it can be made better are vital aspects for maintaining momentum and motivation. Student and virtual teams benefit incredibly by being able to pause and take a look at what they've built. I can't conceive of a way that a team could eliminate or substantially modify the sprint review and still have a successful ScrumButt implementation.

As was discussed before, the sprint retrospective is the meeting that is most frequently dropped by scrum teams with a moderate amount of scrum experience, and it always has detrimental consequences. Teams that are truly scrum experts never eliminate the retrospective, even when their ability to improve productivity reaches the limits of human capacity. Similarly, your team should *never* decide to stop having retrospectives, which will ensure you are always getting the most out of scrum.

The Bottom Line

Getting to see your project in a working state every couple weeks is one of the things that separates scrum from a lot of other project management systems. It is incredibly rewarding and also provides an opportunity to evaluate the product and change priorities if assumptions made early in product development turn out to be wrong.

Having an official meeting to regularly review working habits gives teams the satisfaction of getting more done with the same amount of time and ensures that bad habits don't sneak into the team culture.

ScrumButtThinking

1. If a product owner is surprised by what he sees during the sprint review, what could he do to make sure that future sprints meet his expectations?
2. Can you think of another way to elicit great feedback about the teams' working habits other than SCS?

ScrumButtNOW!

1. Open the ScrumButt Resources workbook.
2. Find the Sprint Retrospective worksheet.
3. Unless it's the last day of your sprint, you can't do anything with it right now. But look at it with appreciation in your eyes.
4. Promise to use it at the end of your sprint.
5. Sing TLC's "I don't want no scrub" but replace the word scrub with scrum. It's funny, but it's not true. You want scrum.

12

Do It!

The great aim of education is not knowledge but action.

Herbert Spencer

Chapter in a Tweet

Do or do not. There is no try.

Well amigos, there is nothing else to know. Thanks for reading. Bye.

OK. OK. I won't lie to you or leave you hanging like that.

There is so much more to know. While agile and scrum principles and practices have been around for decades, they have seen a rapid rise in popularity over the last decade. Yet even people who are considered scrum experts will tell you that they are still learning about scrum, and they expect to continue to learn more for the rest of their lives. If you've enjoyed reading this book, and want to get deeper into scrum in general, or a particular aspect of scrum, there is no shortage of resources and options.

However, I don't think that should be what you do next. If you haven't already, get your hands dirty and put scrum to the test. If you're not currently on a project, assemble a team (get everyone on it a copy of this book), pick your roles, and have at it. You will learn more by doing than you can ever learn by reading alone.

If you're already on a team that is struggling with deadlines and morale, scrum offers a concrete plan for addressing many of the sources of these issues. Don't let feeling like you don't know enough about scrum paralyze you. Take action. Make the leap. Your team will thank you!

Beyond that, I hope you will take some of the philosophies of scrum and apply them to your life. Don't plan too far ahead. Be open to new opportunities as they arise. Always prioritize the most important things. Constantly try to be better.

Good luck in your personal and professional journey.

Noah

Glossary

Burndown: A chart that tracks time on the x-axis and effort remaining in the sprint on the y-axis. Because less effort will remain as time goes on, the chart value goes down or "burns" down.

Ceremony: A meeting prescribed by scrum best practices. Scrum teams may schedule regular meetings in addition to the required ceremony meetings.

Colocation: The practice of having people that work on the same project do their work in the same physical space.

Definition of done: A checklist that describes any quality assurance or other steps a task must go through to be considered complete.

Developer: A member of the scrum team who uses their talents to bring the project to life. In scrum, this term does not refer specifically to a software engineer but includes artists, designers, and anyone who *develops* the project.

Planning poker: A system for estimating tasks by having all team members secretly estimate a task and then reveal their estimates simultaneously.

Product backlog: A prioritized list of the features the product should have. The most important features first. The priority is determined by the product owner.

Product owner: The person responsible for setting the priorities in a scrum project.

Retrospective: A meeting during which the scrum team reflects on their working habits.

Return on investment: The ratio of the rewards for investing in a project vs. the costs of investing in a project. The formula for calculating return on investment (ROI) is

$$\text{Return on investment} = \frac{\text{Gain from investment} - \text{Cost of investment}}{\text{Cost of investment}}$$

The worst possible ROI is –1, meaning you lost all your investment and gained nothing. An ROI of 0 means you gained only enough to recover your initial investment. A positive ROI indicates that your project recuperated its cost along with some amount of profit. The higher the number, the more profitable. ROI is frequently expressed as a percentage (e.g., 1 = 100%).

When calculating ROI, especially on a project that does not require the actual expenditure of funds, it is important to account for your time as a cost.

Scrum coach: A veteran scrum practitioner who can help guide a new scrum team transitioning from other forms of project management.

ScrumMaster: The person on the team who is most focused on making sure that the project follows scrum protocols and who quarterbacks issues that are outside the team's expertise.

SCS: An abbreviation for Start/Commit/Stop, a strategy used during the retrospective for eliciting team feedback about how the team can improve velocity.

Sprint: A predefined interval of time (1–4 weeks) during which the scrum team will work to deliver a working version of the project with the most valuable features implemented.

Sprint backlog: A list of features and associated tasks that will be completed by the team during the next sprint.

Sprint review: A meeting during which the product owner and other stakeholders are shown the results of the most recent sprint, and during which the development team and other stakeholders have an official opportunity to influence the direction of the product by sharing their feelings about how the product owner should prioritize the product backlog.

Story points: A way of measuring the effort to complete a task that doesn't directly make use of man-hours.

User story: A description of a project feature written from the perspective of the target audience.

Velocity: The speed at which work is completed, expressed as work done over time. Most frequently, velocity is discussed in relation to the whole team over the sprint (e.g., 10 story points per sprint), but you can also talk about the velocity of an individual team member.

Whatchu: A humorous abbreviation of "what are you" or "what have you" depending on the context. All of the questions asked during the daily stand-up begin with this phrase.

Index

A

Aligning schedules, 97
Artifact, 40
"As a *blank* I want *blank* so that *blank*"
    (AsABIWaB), 44, 46
Asynchronous teams, 98

B

Burndown chart, 91–94
Business life
    education, 5–6
    before scrum
        blue-printing phase, 4
        competent developers, 3
        documentation, 1
        fixed price, 5
        last-minute integration issues, 5
        marketing, 2
        plain language description, 4
        project management process, 3
        prototypes, 1
        ROI, 2

C

Colocation, 23, 56, 59–60
Conflicting priorities, 32
Cross-functional teams, 54–55, 59

D

Daily stand-up (Daily scrum), 15, 17–18, 87–88
Definition of done (DoD), 73–74
Developer, 53–54, 88–89, 94, 105
Development team
    long-term plan, 87
    self-managing subject matter experts, 23

F

Feedback, 13, 32–33, 36, 42–43, 104

L

Long-term plan
    development team, 87
    responding to change, 16

M

Manifesto for Agile Software Development, 13
Micromanagement, 18, 87

O

Overlapping schedules, 97

P

Performance dropping, 108
Planning session
    product owner feedback, 33
    sprint lengths, 96
Product backlog, 103–104
    artifact, 40
    AsABIWaB, 44–46
    breakdown, 72–73
    capacity, 64–65
    community, 48
    conversations, 64
    DoD, 73–74
    estimating process, 69–72
    estimation problem, 66
    example (gardening), 65–66
    feature list, 41
    highest-priority story, 75–76
    implementing change, 48
    improved information, 43
    logging in, 41
    low-value feature, 43
    physical things, 49
    planning poker, 74–75
    predetermined feature list, 43
    product owner, 41
    project features, 39
    project management systems, 48

ScrumButt modifications, 49–50, 76–78
scrum team, 41–42
sprint planning, 63, 74
story points, 66–69
target audience, 42
team members, 75–76
user interface, 47
user story, 46
waterfall project management, 39–40
Product owner
    AsABIWaB tool, 50
    feature priority, 34
    half-empty perspective
        indecisive, 32–33
        irresponsible, 33
        multiple personalities, 31–32
        plain language priority, 36
        technically minded, 35–36
        unavailable, 33
        unintuitive, 33–34
        unrespectable, 34
    role of, 14
    team tasks, 36
    technical ability, 47

Q

Quality assurance process, 102

R

Return on investment (ROI), 2, 11, 13, 34

S

Scrum
    agile alternatives, 18
    agile manifesto, 13–14
    changes, responding to, 16
    continuous action, 18
    cost-centric project management, 11
    customer collaboration, 15
    customers and costs, 7–8
    individuals and interactions, 14–15
    OCD learning tendencies, 27
    philosophies, 112
    principles of, 24–25
    process, 16

project management, 25
    problems, 8
    values, 18
project sample, 29–31
project solution, 17–18
resources and options, 111
ROI, 13
ScrumButt NOW!, 26
solving problems, non-scrum ways
    detailed contracts and relationship
        managers, 10
    detailed upfront planning and
        estimation, 9
    focus groups, 11
    task relationships and dependencies,
        10–11
    team-building activities, 9–10
    tight employee supervision and
        hierarchies, 9
sprints, 17
waterfall process, 12–13
workflow and style, 26
working software, 15
ScrumButt
    activities, 37
    best practices, 22
    collocation, 23
    examples, 22
    implementations, 22
    individual practices, 23
    minimum requirements, 21
    modificarion, 36
    project management framework, 21
    software development, 21
Scrum coach
    feedback, stakeholders, 104
    prioritization choices, 85
Scrum master, 91–92
    agile manifesto, 81
    checks and balances, 81
    emergency team meetings, 84
    interruption interceptor, 84
    judgment, 82
    judicial branch, 82
    1-on-1 conversations, 107
    problem solver, 83–84
    product owner, 36
    role of, 14
    ScrumButt modifications, 85–86
    scrum coach, 85
    sprint retrospective, 83
    team's effectiveness, 83

team's practices, 109
violations, 82
Scrum team
   AsABIWaB tool, 50
   sprint retrospective, 109
SCS, *see* Start/Continue/Stop (SCS)
Short-term planning
   attendees, 88
   burndown chart, 91–94
   committed/involved team members, 89
   daily stand-up meetings, 87
   effective meeting, 88
   nuclear option, 94–96
   schedule, 94
   ScrumButt, 97–98
   sprint intervals, 98
   Whatchu
      challenges, 91
      less effective task, 90
      more effective task, 90
      productivity, 90
      product owner, 91
      scrummaster, 91
      solutions, 91
      sprint log, 89
      sprint planning, 91
      timely resolution, 91
Silos, 54
SME, *see* Subject matter expert (SME)
Sprint backlog, 92, 96–97
Sprint goals, 87, 94–95
Sprint intervals, 98
Sprint length, 95–96
Sprint log, 64, 89–90
Sprint planning, 95–96
   product owner, 102–103
   stand-up meetings, 102
   story points, 74
Sprint retrospective
   review velocity
      commitments, 105–106
      commit to improvements,
         107–108
      Keep It Up and Keep It Fresh,
         108–109
      SCS, 106–107
   ScrumButt modification, 109
Sprint review
   acceptance, 102–103
   demonstration, 102
   influence, 103–104
   ScrumButt modification, 109

Stakeholders, 44, 50, 104
Stand-up meetings, 88
   product owner, 102
   sprint goals, 87
   team members, 89
   Whatchu, 89–91
Start/Continue/Stop (SCS), 106–107
Subject matter expert (SME), 56, 60
Superhero teams
   colocation, 56, 59
   communication, 57
   cross-functional teams, 59
   developer, 53
   equal collaborator, 55
   flat organizations, 55
   peers, 57–58
   ScrumButt modification, 58–60
   scrum practitioners, 57
   silos, 54
   SME, 56
   sprint time, 60

T

Team capacity, 104
Team culture, 109
Team hierarchy, 60
Team members
   AsABIWaB, 50
   estimating tasks, 75
   print planning sessions, 78
   role of, 14
   scrum master, 14
   self-managing subject matter
      experts, 23

U

User interface, 47–48, 59, 102
User statuses database, 35–36
User story, 46

V

Velocity, 105–109
Virtual teams, 23, 50, 58–60, 97, 109

W

Whatchu
    challenges, 91
    less effective task, 90
    more effective task, 90
    productivity, 90

    product owner, 91
    ScrumMaster, 91
    solutions, 91
    sprint log, 89
    sprint planning, 91
    timely resolution, 91
Working habits, 101, 103, 109